THE
FIRST-TIME
MANAGER

THIRD EDITION

THE
FIRST-TIME
MANAGER

THIRD EDITION

LOREN B. BELKER

amacom

American Management Association

New York • Atlanta • Boston • Chicago • Kansas City • San Francisco • Washington, D.C.
Brussels • Toronto • Mexico City

This publication is designed to provide accurate and authoritative
information in regard to the subject matter covered. It is sold with
the understanding that the publisher is not engaged in rendering
legal, accounting, or other professional service. If legal advice or
other expert assistance is required, the services of a competent
professional person should be sought.

Library of Congress Cataloging-in-Publication Data
Belker, Loren B.
    The first-time manager / Loren B. Belker. -- 3rd ed.
        p.   cm.
    Includes index.
    ISBN 0-8144-7802-6
    1. Supervision of employees. 2. Office management.   I. Title.
HF5549.B355   1993
658.3'02--dc20   92-33135
                                                                        CIP

Printing number

20 19 18 17 16 15 14 13 12 11

For
Darlene,
my wife and my best friend

Contents

Acknowledgments

People often have a greater impact on our lives than they're aware of at the time.

My family has provided endless support and encouragement during all the time I've spent writing this and other books.

I would like to acknowledge my good friend Professor Bill Torrence from the Department of Management at the University of Nebraska, who read an early draft and offered encouragement at a critical time in the writing of the original manuscript.

I want to express my thanks to the late Betty Todd and to Debbie Fisk and Tamar Lasky for their manuscript preparation of the original and revised versions of this book.

Finally, my ongoing gratitude to my wife and best friend, Darlene. I wish I could be just half as great as she thinks I am.

Introduction

So you're going to manage people. Your life will never be the same.

You're embarking on a stage of your career that will be an unending challenge. That challenge will be the achievement of goals or objectives through others. That is what supervision and management are all about.

Application of the principles described here should benefit anyone who is about to embark on a managerial career. Our relationship with other human beings is the most challenging opportunity that exists for us. It covers all aspects of our lives.

There are many books on the subject of management, but few of them address themselves to—or zero in on—those individuals who are about to begin a career of leading others. These people are not interested in a lot of academic claptrap; rather, they are in a state of mixed emotion—absolutely delighted with the promotion and absolutely panic-stricken with the realization that from now on they'll be judged by how well their subordinates perform.

This book is for those people, not for top management with thirty years' experience, even though many top managers would do well to refresh their acquaintance with some of the basic principles that will be discussed.

Since the first edition of this book appeared, I've conducted numerous seminars on the first-time manager. One comment that is made repeatedly by participants is, "I wish my boss would read this book" or "My boss needs this information as much as I do." These comments are made so frequently that I'm led to the conclusion that many experienced managers out there have moved away from the basics. The late football coach Vince Lombardi got back to basics by holding a football in his hands and declaring to his players, "Gentlemen, this is a football." Perhaps when it comes to management, we could paraphrase and say, "Executives, this is a human being."

I've attempted to write this guide in a conversational manner, as if I were talking directly to you. I trust you'll find it easy to refer back to specific areas should problems arise in the future. I strongly recommend that you reread this book after six months' experience of managing other people. Some of the concepts may take on additional usefulness at that time.

Several new chapters have been added in this third edition, and some chapters have been expanded. You will note the important discussion of change, detail, and the big picture; the complex issue of organizational and personal loyalty; the problems a young manager encounters when supervising older employees; making more effective use of the telephone; the crucial role a sense of humor plays in management; and several other key issues for first-time managers.

Thanks for deciding to spend some time with me.

One

The New Kid on the Block

1

How People Are Chosen as Supervisors

Unfortunately, many companies don't go through a very thorough process in choosing those who are to be moved into managerial positions. Often the judgment is based solely on how well the person is performing in the currently assigned task. The best performer doesn't always make the best manager, although many companies still make the choice on that basis. The theory is that successful past performance is the best indicator of future success.

It's important that you have a record of being successful, but being the best operator doesn't make you the best leader, for a number of reasons. If the current job doesn't require that you work cooperatively with others, you could be performing well as a loner.

So the fact that you're a good performer, even though it demonstrates a success pattern, doesn't necessarily mean you'll be successful as a manager. Being a manager requires skills beyond those of being a satisfactory operator.

Some companies have management training programs. These vary from excellent to horrible. Too often the program is given to people who have already been in managerial positions for a number of years. If the program has any merit, it should be given to individuals who are being considered for management positions. This helps them avoid mistakes and also gives the trainees the opportunity to see whether they will be comfortable leading others. Anyone who has worked for any length of time has observed situations where promotions didn't work out and the person asked for the old job back. There's an old cliché that goes like this: "Don't wish too hard for something because you might get it." Some people become so concerned with the gratification of a promotion, with its additional salary, that they don't spend enough time doing a self-analysis about whether they'll be suited for the change in responsibilities.

The Octopus

There are those who really believe that if you want something done right, you'd better do it yourself. People with this attitude rarely make good leaders because they have difficulty delegating responsibility. We've all seen them: They delegate only those trivial tasks that any idiot could perform, and anything meaningful they keep themselves. As a result, they work evenings and weekends and take a briefcase home as well. I'm not putting down overtime, because all of us occasionally must devote some extra time to the job, but people who follow this pattern as a way of life are poor managers. They have so little faith in their subordinates that they trust them with nothing important. What they're really saying is that they don't know how to properly train their people.

There's usually a turnover problem in a section with this kind of manager. The employees are usually more qualified than the "octopus" believes (the term *octopus* is used because such a leader reaches out and takes personal possession of all the responsible tasks), and they soon tire of handling only trivia.

I suspect you know of an octopus in your own office. I hope you're not working for one, because you'll have a difficult time being promoted. Caught up in your impossible situation, you're not given anything responsible to do, and as a result you never get a chance to demonstrate what you can do. You seldom get a recommendation for promotion from Mr. Octopus—assuming for a moment that he's a man. He's convinced that the reason he has to do all the work is his people don't accept responsibility. He can never admit that it's because he refuses to delegate.

Mr. Octopus is a tragedy and should never have been put into a responsible position. When he himself gets passed over for promotion, he becomes quite bitter because no one works harder than he does, and obviously his efforts are not appreciated. There is one basic truth that this person does not understand, which is: Never become irreplaceable, because when you do, you also become unpromotable.

Particular attention has been given to Mr. Octopus, primarily so that you won't allow yourself to fall into this trap. If you do become this kind of monster, it probably follows on your having just received your last promotion up the corporate ladder—unless the top executive is an octopus himself. In that case the whole organization is in trouble, and there's a good chance the top executive will die a premature death. This is not to imply that every executive who dies prematurely is an octopus manager.

One other unvarying trait of a Mr. Octopus is that he seldom takes his vacation all at once. He takes it a couple of days at a time because the company obviously can't continue functioning without him any longer than that. I've known octopus leaders whose retirement years were absolutely demolished because retirement meant abolition of their reason for living, their dedication to the job.

The Chosen Few

In many organizations, new managers are chosen because of the current supervisor's recommendation. If you're fortunate, you're working for such a person. This type of leader gives subordinates a great deal of latitude; as a result, the department achieves a reputation as a breeding ground for future managerial talent. (We'll talk more in Chapter 18 about how you can develop into this kind of manager.)

People are also chosen to head a function because they're related to the boss. Consider yourself fortunate if you're not in such a company. Even if you *are* related to the boss, it's very

difficult to assume additional responsibility under such circumstances. You doubtless have the authority, but today's businesses aren't dictatorships and people won't perform well for
you just because you've been anointed from on high. So, if
you're the boss's son or daughter, you really have to prove
yourself. You'll get surface respect, but let's face it—it's what
people really think of you, not what they say to you, that
matters and that affects how they perform. If you're related to
the boss, you might consider getting your experience elsewhere before taking on a supervisory position in your relative's
firm. Since the vast majority of you are not in that position,
let's see what other problems you face.

In most organizations, you're not chosen for a managerial
position because of your technical knowledge. You're chosen
because someone has seen the spark of leadership in you.
That's the spark you must start developing. Leadership is
difficult to define. A leader is a person others look to for
direction, a person whose judgment is respected because it's
usually sound. As you exercise your judgment and develop the
capacity to make sound decisions, it becomes a self-perpetuating characteristic. Your faith in your own decision-making
power is fortified. That feeds your self-confidence, and with
more self-confidence you become less reluctant to make difficult decisions.

Some of the country's larger corporations do have formal
management programs. Often they recruit people directly out
of college. As a result, many people already in the corporation
who would make great managers if given the opportunity are
frozen out. Many of these programs are well constructed and
broad based. People chosen off the college campus may or may
not make outstanding managers of people. Just as it is a
mistake to assume that a good personal producer will always
make a satisfactory manager of people, so it may be a mistake
to assume that someone placed in a management program will
be a good manager. The advantage of such programs may be
that trainees are not put into positions of supervising people
until they've gone through the training. Such programs are
most successful when they select people from many sources,
including sources within the organization.

A leader is a person who can see into the future and visualize the result of his or her decision making. A leader is also a person who can set aside matters of personality and make decisions based on fact. This doesn't mean you ignore the human element—you never ignore it, but you deal always with the facts themselves, not with people's emotional perception of those facts.

People are chosen to be managers for a wide variety of reasons. If you're chosen for sound reasons, your acceptance by your new subordinates will, for the most part, be much easier to come by.

2

The First Few Months

Your first week on the job as a manager will be unusual, to say the least. If you're a student of human behavior, you'll observe some surprising developments.

Settling In

Don't believe that everyone is happy about the choice of the new kid on the block. Some of your co-workers will feel *they* should have been chosen. They may be jealous of your new promotion and secretly hope you fall on your face.

Others, the office "yes people," will immediately start playing up to you. As the chosen one, you can be their ticket to success. Their objective isn't all bad, but their method of operation leaves something to be desired.

Others will put you to the test early. They may ask you questions to see if you know the answers. If you don't, they'll want to see if you'll admit it or if you'll try to bluff your way through it. Some may ask you questions you can't possibly know the answers to yet, for the sheer delight of embarrassing you.

Most—you hope the majority—will adopt a wait-and-see attitude. They're not going to condemn or praise you until they see how you perform. This attitude is healthy and all you really have a right to expect.

You'll be measured initially against your predecessor in the position. If that other's performance was miserable, yours will look great by comparison even if it's mediocre. If you follow a highly capable performer, your adjustment will be tougher. Before you begin thinking it's best to follow a miserable performer, consider the load of tough problems you're inheriting from your inept predecessor; that's why you're there. The highly capable predecessor is probably gone because he or she was promoted. So, in either case, you have a big job ahead of you.

One of your first decisions should be to refrain from immediately instituting changes in the method of operation. (In abnormal situations, top management may have instructed you to go in and make certain immediate changes because of the seriousness of the situation. However, in such cases it is usually announced that changes will be forthcoming.) Above all, be patient. If you make changes immediately, you'll be resented. Your actions will be construed as arrogance and an insult to your predecessor. Many young new leaders make their own lives more difficult by assuming they have to use all their newfound power immediately. The key word should rather be *restraint*. Whether or not you want to admit it, you're the one who's on trial with your subordinates, not they with you.

This is a good time to make an important point about your own attitude. Many young managers communicate rather well upward to their superiors, but poorly downward to their subordinates. Your subordinates will have more to say about your future than your superiors. You're going to be judged by how well your section or department functions, so the people who now work for you are the most important in your business life. Believe it or not, they're more important even than the president of your company. This bit of knowledge has always seemed obvious to me, yet many new managers spend almost all their time planning their upward communication and give only a passing glance to the people who really control their future.

You undoubtedly know members of the management team who come strolling into the office well after the beginning hour. This is a luxury you can't afford. It's unreasonable to expect subordinates to consider it important to be punctual and start work at the designated time if it's not important to you. Leading by example is still a good concept. This is an area where I recommend that you deviate from your predecessor's practice immediately. Your people will respect you because you observe the same rules that they're expected to observe. The boss who comes in late loses more than the productivity for that hour. That's indeed the smallest part of the lost cost. How do you measure the cost of the halfhearted work that takes place before the top executive comes into the office? It's not that the staff won't work unless they're being watched; rather, they reflect their own manager's attitude. You can't blame them for responding in that manner.

The Personal Touch

Sometime during the first sixty days on the job you should plan on having a personal conversation with each of the people in your area of responsibility. Don't do this the first week or so. Give your subordinates a chance to get used to the idea that you're there. When it comes, the conversation should be formal in nature. Ask your subordinates into your office for an unhurried discussion about anything that's on their mind. Do no more talking yourself than necessary. This first formal discussion is not designed for you to communicate with the others; it's designed to open lines of communication from them to you. (Have you ever noticed that the more you allow the other person to talk, the higher you'll be rated as a brilliant conversationalist?)

Although the employee's personal concerns are important, it's preferable to restrict the discussion to work-related topics. Sometimes it's difficult to define these limits because problems at home may be troubling the employee more than anything else, but at all times you must avoid getting into a situation where you're giving personal advice. Just because you've been anointed as the boss, that doesn't make you an expert on all the personal problems confronting your people. Listen to them; often that's what they need more than anything else—someone to listen to them.

A method I've used in such conversations seems to work rather well. You have to be genuinely interested in people—you can't fake it. The method is to say nothing in the conversation that will tend to terminate it. You must never give the other the sense of being hurried out of the office. For example, the conversation has gone on for only ten minutes and you say, "It sure was great talking to you." The employee will immediately recognize that the statement is meant to terminate the conversation. If your wish to learn what your people are thinking is sincere, you'll avoid what I call *conversation terminators*.

The Conversation Terminator

It may be worthwhile at this point to give further examples of conversation terminators. My purpose is twofold: First, I want you to recognize them when they're used on you; second, I want them to be available for your own use at appropriate times. Although you'll avoid using the device until you're certain the employee you're interviewing has "gotten it all out," it definitely belongs in your management tool chest.

If you've ever had a conversation in someone's office and, while you're talking, watched your host reach over and rest a hand on the telephone receiver even though the telephone hasn't rung, that's a conversation terminator. It says, "As soon as you leave I'm going to make a phone call." Another technique is for the person to pick up a piece of paper from the desk and glance at it periodically during your conversation.

The conversation terminator I particularly like is the one where the host turns in his chair behind the desk to a side position as though about to get up. If that doesn't work, he stands up. That always gets the message across. This approach seems too direct and I personally avoid it, but sometimes it becomes necessary.

It's important that you recognize these conversation terminators. You'll of course try to keep your conversations meaningful enough to preclude their use on you and your use of them on others. There are many more, but you'll compile your own list and find that different people have their own favorite conversation terminators.

Getting to Know Them

Now let's get back to your conversation with your subordinates. The purpose is to give them the opportunity to open communications with you. Show a genuine interest in their concerns; learn what their ambitions are with the company. Ask questions that will get them to expand on their point of view. You can't fake genuine interest in others; you're doing this because you care about the employee's well-being. Such attention is advantageous to both of you. If you can help employees achieve their goals, they'll be more productive; what's more important, they'll feel they're making progress toward their goals.

You'll note that I don't talk about happy employees, because, frankly, I don't know if it's good for a company to have happy employees. Many people think *happy* means satisfied, and a satisfied employee is one who is content. An employee who is content is unlikely to reach out for something better and thus is probably not as productive as she could be.

So your goal in these early conversations is to let your subordinates know you care about them as individuals and you're there to help them achieve their goals. Let them know you want to help them solve whatever problems they may be having with the job. Establish a comfort zone in which they can deal with you. Make them feel that it's perfectly natural for them to discuss small problems with you. By discussing small problems and small irritants, you can probably avoid most of the larger problems.

You'll discover in your first few months as a manager that your technical abilities are not nearly as important as your human abilities. The majority of your problems are going to revolve around the human and not the technical aspects of the job. Unless your responsibilities are technically complex, you'll find that if you have outstanding human skills, you can overlook your minor technical deficiencies. Conversely, even if you're the most technically competent manager in the office, without human skills you'll have great difficulty.

Friends in the Department

One of the problems many new executives confront is handling friendships with people in the department who now become their subordinates. This is a difficult situation and I'm sure there's no perfect answer.

It's obvious that you shouldn't have to give up your friendships simply because you've received a promotion. However, you don't want your friendships to hurt your performance or the performance of your friends.

You can't allow your friendships to interfere with your method of operation. A subordinate who's really a friend will understand the dilemma you find yourself in. It is precisely this dilemma that causes some executives to believe that promoted managers should be brought in from other areas. It minimizes the chances that they'll know their subordinates too well and have close friends within the department.

You must be certain that co-workers who were your friends before you became their supervisor receive the same treatment as everyone else. They must not be treated worse merely to prove to the others how unbiased you are.

If you've usually taken your coffee breaks with certain people in your department, you should consider adopting a rotation policy so that within a short period you'll have had your coffee break with all your subordinates. This practice seems preferable to discontinuing the sessions and going with fellow supervisors. That would be construed as your moving up the corporate ladder: "Her old friends aren't good enough for her anymore." If some of the office friends you meet in a social situation include people you now supervise, you must never allow the discussion to deal with the performance of other people in the department.

It's important that everyone you manage be treated with

equal fairness. Your friends in the department should be treated the same as everyone else. If you do the right kind of job as supervisor, everyone in the department will consider you a friend.

3

Building Confidence

Building confidence is a gradual process. One of your main goals is to develop the confidence of your employees, both in their own abilities and in their opinion of you. They must have confidence that you're competent at your job and that you're fair.

The Success Habit

Building confidence in employees is not an easy task. Do you believe success is habit forming? Failure can also become a habit. Confidence is built on success, so give your people horses they can ride. Especially in dealing with new employees, assign them tasks they can master. Build in them the habit of being successful, starting small with small successes.

Occasionally a subordinate will perform a task incorrectly or just plain blow it. How you handle such situations has a great impact on the confidence of employees. Never correct them in front of others. "Praise in public, criticize in private," the old credo goes—it still has a lot of management truth in it.

Even when you talk to a subordinate in private about an error, your function is to train that person to recognize the nature of the problem so as not to make the same error again. Your attitude about errors will speak louder to an employee than the words you use. Your statements must be directed toward correcting the misunderstanding that led to the error and not toward personal judgment. Never say or do anything that will make the employee feel inadequate. You want to build confidence, not destroy it. If you get pleasure from making subordinates feel foolish, then you'd better start examining your own motives, because you can't build yourself up by tearing someone else down. Examine the error on the basis of what went wrong, where the misunderstanding occurred, and go on from there. Treat the small error routinely; don't make it bigger than it really is.

Let's briefly discuss the "praise in public" part of the old credo. I used to believe in that concept until I found that it too sometimes created problems. The individual on the receiving end of the praise felt warm and fuzzy about the compliment, but others who were not so commended reacted negatively. The disappointment was then directed at the employee who was praised. That's why it's important to be cautious about praising in public. "Good work" and "I appreciate the great job you did on this" are about as far as you can go without creating a problem for the person you're attempting to reward. Why make life tougher for that employee by creating jealousy or resentment in the people he must work with eight hours a day? If you really want to praise someone expansively for outstanding performance, do it in the privacy of your office. You'll get the pluses without the negatives of resentment and jealousy from co-workers.

You can also build confidence by involving your people in some of the decision-making processes. Without delegating any of your supervisory responsibilities to them, allow them to have some major input into matters that affect them. A new task about to be performed in your area presents the opportunity to give your subordinates some input. Solicit ideas from them on how the new task might best be worked into the daily routine. Given this kind of participation, the new routine will succeed because it's everyone's routine, not just yours. This doesn't mean your staff is making decisions for you; what I'm suggesting is that by involving your people in the process that leads up to your decision, you'll have them working with you rather than accepting new systems imposed on them.

The Evils of Perfectionism

Some managers expect perfection from their employees. They know they won't get it but they feel they'll get closer to it by demanding it. Unfortunately, some executives really believe they can get perfection from employees. By insisting on perfection you may in fact defeat your own purposes: Some employees will become so self-conscious about making a mistake that they slow their performance down to a crawl to make absolutely certain they don't screw up. As a result, production goes way down. The company might be better off having a production of one hundred with five errors than a production of twenty with one error.

Another drawback to being a perfectionist is that everyone resents you for it. Your subordinates believe you're impossible to please and you prove it to them every day. You know what the acceptable standards for work performance are in your company; no one can blame you for wanting to be better than the average; but you'll have far more success if you get the employees involved in helping decide how to improve performance. If it's their plan, you have a significantly better chance of achieving your goal.

You can also build confidence by developing esprit de corps within your own area. Make sure, however, that the feeling you build is supportive of the prevailing company spirit and not in competition with it.

The Limitations of Power

During the 1930s, when unemployment was high, companies demanded respect for executives, and employees adhered to company methods and procedures without question. I suppose there are still some managers around who'd love to be able to issue orders and have their every wish carried out as though they were back in "the good old days." It takes a highly qualified person to be a leader in today's business world, where instructions are questioned and more time is spent persuading than issuing dictatorial orders. Only rarely should the enlightened manager have to reach back and use naked power to get things done.

There are some who believe that if you have the power, you use it. The enlightened manager seldom uses power, not from fear of using it, but because its use is unnecessary. You don't have to go around with a sign on your lapel that says BOSS. Everyone knows you're in charge; issuing orders unnecessarily merely adds an aggressive element: "I'm boss and you better believe it!" Managers who are most successful in dealing with others seldom reach back and use the authority they have. They're able to get the job done without "pulling rank." If the only way you can get routine jobs done is to use all the authority you have, what are you going to do when you have a serious problem?

Attitudes are discussed at length in Chapter 10. Your own attitude is important in building confidence. Your subordinates can sense more about your attitude than you suspect. They learn to understand your moods and they find out where your triggering mechanisms are. Therefore, work to be consistent in your behavior so that your employees aren't continually surprised by your fluctuating attitudes and actions.

You'll find that your concern for and efforts toward building your employees' confidence will do a great deal in fortifying your own self-confidence. It's similar to the old cliché about the teacher gaining the most from a learning experience. However, this isn't the only way to build your own confidence.

You also build it by making correct decisions. Each time you score well with a solid decision, confidence in your ability to make judgments is reinforced.

Decision Making

This naturally leads to the subject of decision making. Some people agonize over every decision they have to make. If making decisions is a constant irritation for you, you should seriously consider getting out of management. Life is too short to be spent in a state of turmoil every day. There are surely plenty of jobs that are challenging and financially rewarding and that require talent, but not the talent to make decisions.

I see two basic reasons why some people have trouble making decisions. First, they're not sure they have all the information necessary to make a decision; second, they're afraid of making a mistake and having to suffer its consequences.

It's unlikely that you'll ever be able to gather 100 percent of the information that might apply to a given business situation. Even if you think you have all there is, you could find a new bit of information a few days later that proves otherwise. If you've been reasonable and prudent in gathering the information you need, even though spending more time might get you that last 5 percent, go ahead and make the decision. It's highly unlikely that having that additional 5 percent would have led you to a different judgment.

It goes without saying that you'll blow one once in a while. All you're after is to be correct most of the time. I won't use the cliché about the baseball player who bats .300—in business you can't afford to make correct judgments only three times out of ten. That would mean being wrong seven times out of ten. As you get more experience you'll find that you're making correct decisions 99 percent of the time, because in most situations the answer is obvious and you're being asked to reinforce someone else's judgment. Many problems are brought to you because a subordinate wants your agreement and approval before proceeding. Entire books have been written about the decision-making process. Common sense will provide the correct answer in most managerial situations. If you remember nothing else that's been said so far about the decision-making process, remember this: You can get into more management difficulty by repeatedly refusing to make decisions than by occasionally making an incorrect one.

4

The "We and They" Syndrome

"I don't know why *they* made that rule."

"*They* certainly don't understand the people on the firing line."

"If *they* only knew how *we* feel about such practices."

"I don't know what *we* can do about it when *they* issue such dumb regulations."

* * *

You can come up with many more examples. The "we and they" syndrome indicates a state of mind that regards *they* as the enemy. Who *they* are depends on who *you* are. *They* can include all those who are one level or more above you, or it can be restricted to the top management of the company. *We* is you and anyone you consider a peer.

Now that you're a manager you might as well accept the fact that you're part of the *they* you and your peer group used to talk about when you were still a member in good standing of the *we*. You're not going to be able to make the *we* and *they* disappear because of your promotion. To some members of the *we* you're a traitor because you crossed over and became a member of the *they*.

The largest restraint placed on members of the *we* group is the limitation that exists in their own minds. Recognition of the "we and they" syndrome is important. It puts the action of many people in its proper perspective.

Many recently promoted managers fall prey to the feeling that they're still in a *we* group, but that the *we* is now their own management group. In other words, it's a switch of labels. Don't fall into this trap. Rise above this kind of thinking. From now on, there should be only the single *we* group that includes everyone in the organization.

You won't change everyone. You may not change anyone but yourself. But you're the most important person under your control and that's a solid beginning. You can at least put your own thinking in its proper perspective. Perhaps we have hold of a great truth here. Maybe the problems of this planet could be reduced if more of its inhabitants would start thinking in terms of *we* instead of *they*.

The thought may enter your mind that I am describing an attitude that goes beyond the question of management. That may be true. But your job is so large a part of your life, and it spills over into so many other aspects of your daily activities, that the point is worth making.

5

Use of the Possessive

Many new managers, and unfortunately many not so new, have the bad habit of using the possessive as it relates to staff. They say *"my* staff," *"my* department," *"my* assistant," and *"my* secretary."

Even if nothing is meant by this tendency, it is a bad one. It indicates ownership or a proprietary interest, and it is a tip-off of an improper attitude toward the people who report to you. You do not own the department, the assistant, or the secretary.

There are times when you cannot avoid such usage. If you're in a meeting with fellow-managers and your boss, and the boss asks "How's the expense control in your department?" he's making an identification, not suggesting ownership. Likewise, there are other times when using the possessive avoids awkward or misleading statements. In this book, for instance, I refer to "your staff," or "your employees" for identification purposes only; it doesn't imply ownership. In these situations, the possessive is not an ego trip. But for the most part, try to avoid language that implies you own your staff.

A number of years ago, a friend told me that he'd had lunch with a mutual friend at the University Club. When I asked who it was, he mentioned my boss's name. I said, "Oh, I work for Jim."

"He never mentioned that," my friend replied. "He said that you were an associate of his. In fact, he mentioned that your office was right next door to his. He said he really enjoyed working with you."

He *was* my boss. His office *was* next to mine, and about twice as large. But he called me his "associate," and indicated he "enjoyed working" with me. That's not only completely free of ego, but it's a class act. After all these years, the story still brings a smile to my face and a warm feeling toward my ex-boss.

Go and do likewise.

6

Change: Moving From Details to the Big Picture

In 1826, Ludwig Borne said, "Naught endures but change." To put that into today's language, it means, Nothing is as constant as change. How the manager handles aspects of change is covered in other sections of this book, but your overall attitude toward change is critical here. Change in this context means change for you: a move from detailed work to managing others.

The Manager's View of Change

Most people resist change. In an office, almost everyone wants things to stay the way they are. So it is no surprise that some new managers display a split personality when it comes to change. They are intolerant of any resistance to change by subordinates, but display the same resistance when faced with changing their own activities. Advancement into management is a form of change. You need to know what is involved and what qualities are required so you can make that change with grace and style.

Upward or Outward Change

Some bright managers look at the positions one step above them, and say to themselves, "Those people are my age, or

younger. There is no opportunity for me in this company."
They view the organization as static, and see no positive
changes in their future. But this is seldom the case. People
leave unexpectedly for a variety of reasons; others get promoted or advance through a reorganization. So instead of
viewing your company as frozen in time, believe that if something can change, it probably will. Human beings are an
unpredictable lot, and companies are peopled by unpredictable
human beings.

From the Detailed to the General

As you move into management, you will need to be more
involved in the big picture. As a detail person, you probably
handled just one element of an intricate process, and you knew
everything about that one part of the operation. You had depth
of know-how.

But as you move into managing multiple operations, your
know-how has to broaden, and you have to become aware of
how things fit together and why. You can no longer get as
deeply involved in the details. As you move up the organizational ladder, your breadth of know-how increases, and the
depth of detailed operations becomes less important. Yet, you
still know how it all works—the better to manage it. You are
now concerned with completing the puzzle, rather than finding
out how two or three pieces fit together. Some new managers
hang on to the detail they enjoy, but you must resist that
temptation and broaden your management abilities to ensure
your future growth in the organization.

Pitfalls for the New Manager

Most first-time managers do not supervise a large group of
people. Therefore, there may be a temptation to get too involved in the work of your six or seven people. As you move
up the corporate ladder, you will be responsible for more and
more workers. It is impossible to be involved in the detail work

of thirty-five people, so begin now to distance yourself from the details of each task and concentrate on the overall project.

One of the dangers for a first-time manager is that you now may be managing someone who does your old job, and you may consider it more important than tasks you did not perform. It's human nature to think that what we do is more important than what others do, but that doesn't work when you're the manager. It is not a balanced approach to management.

Likewise, don't make your former detail job into an "occupational hobby." A chemist by profession moved up the corporate ladder, and eventually became the chief executive officer of his chemical company. Since a CEO can make changes in office facilities at whim, this one did. He had a small lab built off his presidential office so he could "tinker" around in his lab when he wanted to. This may or may not be a true story, but it makes an excellent example of the unholy love of detail turning into a refusal to move on.

Often, your first managerial job is a lead operator position. You manage others, but you still have tasks of your own to perform; you wear two hats. If this is your situation, you must stay interested and involved in the detail for a while. But when you move into a full-time management position, don't take an occupational hobby with you, lest it distract you from the bigger picture.

Of course, don't carry this advice to the extreme. When some people move into management, they refuse to help their staff at a "crunch and crisis" time. They read management journals while their staff is frantic meeting deadlines; they are now "in management." That is just plain stupid. You can build great rapport with your staff if, at crunch time, you roll up your sleeves and help resolve the crisis.

A Balanced Viewpoint

In all management matters, maintain a sense of balance. I have a friend who says, "I'm a big-picture guy; don't bother me with the details." But he says this when he's overlooked some serious element that is likely to impede the project at hand. He's joking, but many managers are not. They become so big-picture–oriented that they are oblivious to the details that bring the picture together. They also may be insensitive to how much effort is required to complete the detailed work.

Other managers, including many first-time managers who may have been promoted from a line position, are so enthralled with detail that the overall objective is lost. It's "not being able to see the forest for the trees." Balance is required.

7

Looking Above and Below

We all know people who relate and communicate very well upward and maybe even sideward in an organization, but very poorly downward to their subordinates. (*Upward*, *sideward*, and *downward* are of course references to standings on the organizational chart.)

If I get only one idea across to you in this chapter, the effort will be worth it. The thought is that your subordinates have more control over your future than your superiors. This seems perfectly obvious, but it's amazing how many managers ignore it. They'll write great memos to their boss but do a rotten job of communicating with their own people.

Your promotability will be determined not on the basis of how well you may fit into the new job or what your prospects of success in it are but on how well you perform it. Even if you're satisfied with your current position, you'll be more content performing it well than performing it poorly.

Genuine Concern

One way to perform your job well is to give full attention to the needs of the people in your area of responsibility. Some leaders make the mistake of thinking that the concern they show for their subordinates will be interpreted as a sign of weakness.

Genuine concern, indeed, is a sure sign of strength. Showing interest in the welfare of your people doesn't mean you'll "cave in" to unreasonable demands. Unfortunately, many new executives fail to recognize this. They're unable to differentiate between concern and weakness.

Your concern must of course be genuine. You can't fake it. By genuine concern I mean seeing that your people are properly challenged, and that they're appropriately rewarded when they perform well.

You can't start off by complacently telling yourself, "I'm going to be Mr. Nice Guy." You must seriously take on the burden of responsibility for these people. In fact, you and your team are mutually responsible to one another. Your subordinates now look to you for leadership. You must see to it that the objectives of the company and the objectives of your subordinates are not at cross-purposes. Your people should realize that they can achieve their own objectives only by doing their part in helping the company achieve its overall goals.

The person they look to for leadership is you. You serve as interpreter for the employee. What is the company's policy? You'd better be certain that you know what it is!

Showing Fairness

Another of your responsibilities is to make sure that work in your area is fairly and properly distributed so that no one is being carried along by the others or is doing more than a reasonable share of the carrying. In many offices, work assignments will vary; in others, nearly everyone will perform the same function. The supervisory task in the latter situation is much easier as far as equality of workload is concerned. It has other problems, however, in that relationships among the employees are likely to be more strained. Too many of the people will then spend their time worrying about distribution of work down to a gnat's eyelid. You don't have to be that exact. Your approach should be equitable without being scientifically equal.

I think it's more interesting to manage a section (unit,

division, department) in which a wide variety of tasks are performed. You'll receive a variety of questions ranging from the routine clerical inquiry to the more complex professional one. The questions are important to the questioner, so you should give attention to all of them. You've probably seen the card in many executive offices: "Go ahead and ask your dumb question. It's easier to handle than a dumb mistake."

Variety Among Your Subordinates

You'll find people in your area who aren't interested in promotion. One reason is that they don't want to be responsible for the actions of others. Such people, however, might be interested in being promoted if the new position doesn't require supervising others. Many employees want to be responsible only for themselves, and their kind of personality is also needed in business and industry. The business environment would be rather chaotic if everyone were highly oriented toward managing everyone else.

In dealing with people who prefer not to work closely with anyone else, by all means put them in situations where their performance depends only on themselves. Some people are loners all the way. Then there are the *work loners*, who want to be left alone when it comes to the job but who are not necessarily antisocial. They'll go for coffee with their co-workers, have lunch with them, and even see them socially away from the office. Many workers respond best to the team approach. They need to feel they're part of a unit, and they'll develop great loyalty to their team. They'll perform well if you can put them into a team situation.

It's obvious that you can't get everyone into the ideal situation, but knowing that different people have different approaches to their work will make you a more effective manager. In other words, get people into situations where they're comfortable and you'll get a better performance from them.

Dealing With Your Superiors

I've spent some time talking about your attitude toward your subordinates; it's only proper to pay attention also to your attitude toward your superiors. Your future success indeed depends more on your subordinates than on your superiors, but it would be disastrous to ignore those who outrank you.

If you've just had a big promotion, you're feeling grateful to your boss. You're also pleased that the top exec was perceptive enough to have recognized the talent you have. But your new responsibility demands a new level of loyalty from you. After all, you're now a part of the management team. You can't be a good team member without identifying with the team.

Remember, however, that someone who is your superior in the company isn't necessarily smarter than you. Your boss may be more experienced than you, may have been with the company longer, may have come from the right family, or may be in the top position for other reasons. But it's also possible that your boss performed exceedingly well and is indeed smarter than you.

Loyalty to Them

Loyalty has fallen into widespread disrepute. Blind loyalty has never had much to recommend it, but being loyal doesn't mean selling your soul to the devil. Your company and your boss are not out to rip off the world. If they are, they're not worth being loyal to. More important, you shouldn't be working for them.

So let's assume you're convinced that your company's purpose is commendable and you're pleased to be associated with its goals. The kind of loyalty we're talking about has to do with carrying out policies or decisions you morally support. Your position with your company, let's again assume, allows you some input into decisions having to do with your own area of responsibility. You must make every effort to see that such input is as thoughtful and as broadly based as possible. Don't be the kind of narrow-sighted executive whose recommendations are designed to benefit only his or her own area of responsibility. When this happens, it won't be long before your advice isn't sought because it's too parochial.

If you make recommendations that are broadly based and represent the greater good of the company, your advice will be sought more often. This doesn't mean you're continually offering up your own people as sacrificial lambs. Keep everything in balance. The important thing is your involvement in the decision-making process beyond your own managerial level.

Occasionally a decision or policy will be made that's directly contrary to the opinions you've expressed; you'll be expected to support that decision or policy, and you may even have to implement it. Ask your boss why the decision was made, if you don't already know. Find out what important considerations went into formulation of the policy. Determine what you can about the processes that led to the decision.

The old idea that you follow the leader blindly no longer holds. That kind of loyalty was common during the Great Depression, when jobs were scarce and everyone who held a job wanted desperately to keep it. You can no longer bark orders and expect others to obey without question. We should be grateful that this approach no longer applies because today's more democratic approach requires people to be better managers. Nonetheless many managers and supervisors doubtless wish blind loyalty still existed.

If you're to do an outstanding job of supervision, you have a right to understand the reasons behind major company decisions and company policy. Perhaps your own manager is one who follows higher authority blindly and guards information about top management as if all of it were top secret—and you're the enemy. In that case you may have to be a lot more political in how you go about getting the answers to your questions.

If it's a policy that affects other departments, you can find out from people at your own organizational level in those departments. If a friend in Department X has a boss who shares information freely with subordinates, it may be relatively simple to find out what you want to know over a cup of coffee with your friend.

Dealing With an Unreasonable Boss

It would be naïve to believe that all bosses will be understanding and supportive. At some time in your career, you may be in the uncomfortable position of reporting to someone who is not only difficult to work with but unpleasant to be around. Your boss may be technically competent but unreasonable, and therefore impossible to work for. Unfortunately, you can't fire an incompetent or unreasonable boss, as pleasant as that prospect may be.

There may be several reasons why your boss is difficult to get along with. Perhaps she's miserable because she's sixty years old and feels trapped in a job from which there appears to be no escape.

Her salary may be so good that she can't afford to retire or just quit and seek a career that she'd like. A few executives would like to be like Paul Gauguin, the painter who left France and his family behind to escape to Tahiti, but they may be too responsible to bail out. As a young manager, you may have trouble understanding this.

Of course, even if an executive has reasons for feeling trapped, there is no justification for mistreating you—or anyone else, for that matter.

Some executives are extremely goal-oriented. They could be called aggressive, hard drivers, or even combative. They are bound and determined to achieve their objectives regardless of cost, which sometimes can be exceedingly high. It may cost them a health-shortened life, but meanwhile they make life intolerable for anyone who has to deal with them. Fortunately, more and more companies are recognizing that good human relations are also good business. Enlightened companies send executives for sensitivity training or to seminars on avoiding stress or to courses that teach them how to deal with people more effectively. Unfortunately, when there's a downturn in the economy, one of the first things that some companies cut are these human relations efforts. This sends a rather direct message: "During this period of a tight job market, good human relations are not important to this organization."

There is some evidence that major changes in a person's

personality are not likely to be made. If an executive is hard-nosed and difficult, conversion to Mr. Congeniality is unlikely; nevertheless some improvement can be made, and perhaps the rough edges can be buffed.

If executives walk on people, the organization must bear much of the responsibility. What does a chief executive *do* (don't tell me what he *says*)? When executives are permitted to treat employees like so much fodder, that means that the chief executive either condones such behavior or doesn't know what's going on, which is almost as bad. It's the business of a CEO to acknowledge such things.

I knew an executive who was an enigma wrapped in a cloud of contradiction. He treated his employees like dummies who knew nothing. He always knew what was best, and he seemed to always want to argue. No matter what position they took, he'd take the opposite point of view and argue it to the point of exhaustion. The contradiction appeared during performance appraisals. His salary recommendations were fair, and even bordered on being generous. It was as though he tried to make up for his rotten behavior in this manner. Needless to say, he was Mr. Warmth and Accommodation in dealing with his superiors.

The key question is, What do you do when you realize that you are working for an unreasonable boss? If you conclude that the situation is intolerable and no improvement seems likely, you should seek employment elsewhere. *Elsewhere* might be in another department in the same company, or it might be in some other organization.

The first thing to do is determine if you are overreacting. Ask yourself these questions:

1. Have you given this job a fair test? Have you been on the job long enough to make such a judgment?
2. Is your reaction an emotional one?
3. Did the boss treat your predecessor as badly as you're being treated?
4. Is there any indication that the poor relationship is temporary in nature?

5. Have you done anything to cause such an undesirable relationship?
6. Is the job market such that you can easily find another comparable job?

I'm going to comment on the sixth question first. Perhaps, it's because of my own experiences and environment, but I don't believe you should quit one job until you've found another except when your health is threatened or you're asked to do something illegal or immoral. Once you've decided to leave a job and seek another one, much of what bothered you seems less irritating, because you know (you're the only one who does) that the problem is now temporary.

Now for my comments on the other five questions:

1. *Have you given the job a fair test?* Perhaps you haven't been on the job long enough to make this judgment. In your anxiety over the new job, perhaps you're accentuating negative occurrences in the day's activities because you're so uptight yourself. Tension on a new job is often self-inflicted. I can recall going home with a backache every night during the first two weeks on a new job. The backache was caused by my own tension. So ask yourself if the situation is likely to be better once you've had some experience on the job.

2. *Is your reaction an emotional one?* Is the reaction valid, or does it stem from the stress of being on a new job? Is the reaction personal? Would it seem valid to you if you observed it in someone else?

3. *Did the boss treat your predecessor as badly as you're being treated?* This question should not be too difficult to answer. Other managers are likely to know how your predecessor was treated. If you've been promoted from within, you should already know; office grapevines do a great job of communicating about difficult bosses. If your immediate predecessor has a hand in your orientation, you can find out almost instantly. Unfortunately, you will not have access to this information if your boss is new to the company.

4. *Is there any indication that the poor relationship is temporary*

in nature? This, too, can be answered by determining how predecessors in the job were treated. Perhaps the first two or three weeks were hectic, and then the boss and the new manager settled into a normal working relationship. Unfortunately, some bosses will put a new manager through hell just to see what they are made of, a situation not unlike boot camp. I think it's an unhealthy practice; it may be necessary in the military, where people have to be conditioned to obey immediately because of life-threatening situations, but that is hardly the proper scenario for an office. If four or five of your predecessors all asked for transfers within a short period of time, you have a legitimate reason for demanding to know why this information was withheld from you.

5. *Have you done anything to cause such an undesirable relationship?* If your boss has never had a person in your position last more than a few months, obviously it is not your mistake. However, if the boss has had a satisfactory relationship with previous managers, then what is the problem now? Are your skills satisfactory? If it's lack of knowledge of *this* job, you have a right to be given a reasonable amount of time to learn the position and get a firm hold on the job.

If you conclude that it's nothing you have done (or failed to do), decide what to do about it. Most companies have a policy whereby anyone can go to human resources/personnel with any office problem he feels cannot be settled in his own area. I don't think a new manager ought to take this step too quickly, but if you've done your best to handle the situation and feel you need help, a talk with an HR professional may be the right move.

Two
The End of the Honeymoon

8

Changing the Employee

Some psychologists maintain that the only way people change is through a traumatic experience, a religious conversion, or brain surgery. Whether or not this assertion is true, it does point to the difficulty we encounter if we expect to make basic changes in someone's personality. It's like the woman who marries an alcoholic because she feels it's her mission in life to change him. She may indeed change him if she's a traumatic experience for him.

Basic personality doesn't really change. Making slovenly workers meticulous is probably going to be an impossible task. You can smooth out "minor bumps" in behavior and cause people to modify their actions on the job, but you probably can't create a permanent personality change.

Accommodation

Rather than try to change people, you should attempt to put them in situations where they already have the traits essential for performing the task well. If a particular job requires a perfectionist, you certainly don't fill the position with a person who hates details and then experiment with behavior modification to get a satisfactory performance. You're much better off assigning the job to someone who has not only demonstrated skill with details but enjoys such work. I'll talk more about this in Chapter 10, on hiring employees.

There are simple and effective ways to accommodate an

employee. Transfer the employee to a job that's more in keeping with her capacities. Too often people are moved through
an organization in a rigid line of succession. And too often
managers don't consider that they may be removing subordinates from their comfort zone. Usually, jobs become broader in
nature as they become more important. People who like detail,
who cross every *t* and dot every *i*, are usually uncomfortable
when they move away from such detail. It is fortunate that
there are people who like such trivia, who'll clean up after
some of us "big picture" hotshots. To paraphrase a psychologist I know, "Show me a person with a lot of drive and I'll
show you a nit-picking perfectionist following behind and
cleaning up the mess."

Both types of personalities are needed in an organization.
Don't expect your employees to handle all aspects of their job
perfectly. They'll do better with those elements of the job they
like than with those they dislike. I always try to do those things
first that I dislike so that I can get them out of the way and
spend the rest of the day doing the things I like.

Has it ever occurred to you that most of the problems in a
working environment are related to the attitude of people
toward the work and toward each other? We spend endless
time trying to make our co-workers conform to our idea of
what they ought to be. This is a complete waste of effort. We
ought to attempt instead to put people in jobs where they can
develop their natural traits and their natural preferences. Just
because *we're* interested in promotion, we assume everyone
else is. In our grandiose "Horatio Alger" business environment, we assume everyone wants to move up the ladder and
become the boss.

That is not true. Many people merely want to do their job;
they want to be responsible for no one besides themselves, and
they want to be able to forget the workplace when they walk
out of it at night. They get their reward and their challenge
from other things. Most people rate family ahead of job, health
ahead of job, spiritual well-being ahead of job; many rate
hobbies and recreational interests ahead of job. They perform
satisfactorily on the job but turn off when you talk about more
responsibility and a golden opportunity to move up the ladder.

Natural Followers

We meet people who say they want to be promoted, because getting ahead has been so drilled into the American subconscious that to admit they don't want to get ahead almost makes them un-American. So people mouth the words and nod their heads at the appropriate moments, but in their secret hearts they don't want to be promoted. They don't want to accept more responsibility. They tip you off in many ways—you have to be perceptive enough to pick up the clues. They'll avoid any task that requires joint work. If they do take on joint work, they'll do most of it themselves because only then can they be sure it's done correctly. Or they'll wash their hands of the entire matter and let the other person do 90 percent of the work.

In group meetings such people will seldom offer ideas. When pumped for their thoughts, they'll say little that will commit them to anything of substance. They don't stick out their neck. They realize that sticking out their neck means running the risk that someone may try to chop it off. That hurts, and these people don't want to be hurt. They're the salt of the earth, and American industry would be dead without them. If everyone wanted to be promoted into the executive ranks, the competition would be so tough that you and I would perhaps never make it. We should thank our lucky stars every night that not everyone wants our job. To be effective, a leader must have people to lead, and the people I've been describing make great followers.

A Last Resort: Dismissal or Transfer

Another way to accommodate employees is to replace them. This could amount to an outright dismissal or a transfer to another area of the company. It's a procedure we should spend some time developing. Too often, in large offices, managers unload their problem employees onto another department through the promotion route. When asked by the manager of that other department how the prospective promotee is performing in the current job, they're not completely candid in their reply. I think the only correct policy in this situation is to be completely candid. Someday you yourself may be looking at people in other departments as candidates for promotion into your own department and your best guarantee of not getting someone else's rejects is never to deliver that kind of cheap shot yourself.

I actually had that happen to me once. After we had reviewed personnel department performance appraisals of people one level below the job we were attempting to fill in our division, we ended up with three likely candidates. As is customary, I called the supervisors of these candidates and got a glowing report about one in particular, a man. We promoted him to our department and he ended up being a complete disaster. We had to terminate him after a short period of time because he wasn't doing the job. I then confronted the person who had made the recommendation and asked for an explanation, never dreaming I had been mousetrapped. The answer I got was that the employee had not been satisfactory but might become so if given another opportunity. By not being candid, they tricked me into doing their dirty work for them.

There's of course a great temptation to pay back such a department in kind, but the solution is to make sure no one ever does that to you in the first place. Retaliation in an intercompany operation is not beneficial to anyone.

Rehabilitation

There'd be nothing wrong, however, in attempting to rehabilitate a nonproductive employee if it were done with the full knowledge of everyone involved. In the situation where I was victimized, for example, had my fellow manager sat down with me and indicated that the employee was not doing a good job *but* there were strong reasons for wanting him to have another chance, I might have taken the man. I've known of such trials that have been successful. The work and the worker were not a good fit, but the worker had talent; the move to another area where that talent could be used turned a less than satisfactory employee into a productive one.

Generally, however, you'll be much more effective as a leader if you can solve your own problems in your own department and not unload them onto another department. Companies use many testing devices to put people on jobs that are natural for them, or at least to place them in working areas of some personal preference. These devices range from simple five-minute tests to complex three-hour psychological evaluations. This is something your company either already has or should consider having. To emphasize my point again, you must always be conscious of the advantages of fitting employees to jobs at which they have the best chance of being successful. It's much easier to move people around into jobs that are natural for them than to force them into jobs they perform poorly and then try to "educate" them. It just doesn't work. Some psychologists think major changes in our personalities are unlikely to occur after age 16.

Serious Personal Problems

Some subordinates have personal problems that hinder their attendance and their performance on the job. You would be quite naïve to believe that alcohol, drugs, or serious family difficulties were not going to affect your management responsibilities.

Just because you're a manager doesn't mean you're equipped to handle every problem that comes your way. Many enlightened companies recognize this fact and have established employee assistance programs. These programs are usually community supported, unless the company is large enough to justify an on-site service. Employee assistance programs have professional resources available, have connections with chemical dependency programs, and know all the services that exist within the community.

It's foolish for you as a manager to believe that you have the capacity and the resources to solve any and all problems. If you try to handle a situation beyond your professional competence, you run the risk of making the situation worse. Amateurs have failed for years in dealing with alcoholics. As a manager, your responsibility is to see that the job gets done within the boundaries of sound management principles. The employee's alcohol or drug problem is interfering with accomplishing that objective. Although rescuing a human being is also a legitimate objective, you're swimming in uncharted waters.

You will probably need to have a direct confrontation with the problem employee, but you will have to define your *overall* objective first. Your objective is to straighten out a "work problem." You need to insist that troubled employees solve their problem, and you can even direct them to the employee assistance program. You have to make it clear that if they choose not to solve the problem, they will be dismissed from employment. Take care not to do this in a cruel, uncaring way, but be sure to be firm so there is no misunderstanding. People who are hooked on alcohol or drugs can be the greatest con artists in the world. They'll fake you right out of your socks if you're not careful.

You must be willing to listen, but not to the extent that problem employees spend a great deal of time in your office talking when they should be working. There's a fine line between being a good listener and allowing people to get away from their work for two hours while they drink coffee and pour out all their problems to you.

I don't mean to imply that alcohol and drugs are the only kinds of personal problems you will encounter. Sooner or later in your management career you'll hear of every conceivable problem (including inconceivable problems). People are involved in the totality of life; they have problems with spouses, children, parents, lovers, co-workers, themselves, religion, diets, feelings of self-worth, and so on.

A cardinal rule in dealing with human frailties, one that will save you endless aggravation, is *don't pass judgment*. Solve the work problem, and point employees to where they can solve their personal problems. In some cases you may demand that they solve the problem because of what the failure to find a solution is doing to the work environment.

Don't pass judgment and life will remain worth living.

Individual Style: Benefits and Detriments

Whenever possible, allow your subordinates to individualize the job as much as they can while still maintaining the quality, quantity, and objectives that have to be maintained to achieve company goals. The more you can allow your people to bring their own personality into the job, the better the chance of their being successful at it. The higher the position on the organization chart, the greater the latitude usually allowed for individual styling of that position.

Although it's important that you allow your subordinates to mold the job to their own personality, you have to keep them from riding their own occupational hobbyhorses. Some people will put an overwhelming emphasis on things they like to do, but these may not represent your own priorities in that particular situation. In every job, certain tasks are more important than others. As long as you and the employee agree about the relative importance of certain tasks and attend to them in that order of priority, you won't have a problem. You will have a problem when tasks you consider important are considered unimportant by the employee. You're then working in the reverse order of importance called for by the job. Too often we do the things we like to do first and continually put off doing disagreeable tasks. But in business the supervisor's order of priority always takes precedence over an employee's. Chapter 19, "Organizing Your Own Time," may be helpful in clarifying these matters.

Priorities

One of the biggest errors executives make is in not letting their employees know what work is considered the most important from the company's point of view. They take the attitude that it's all important. That puts employees in the position of deciding what should be done at what time. You can't then blame your subordinates if their sense of priorities ends up different from your own. You must discuss the situation with each employee, and of course the best time to have such a discussion is when the employee first moves into the job.

Subtle shifts repeatedly occur in defining the work load and its importance; to keep your sense of priorities up to date, you have to make sure you and your subordinates are constantly on the same wavelength.

It has often been said that people resist change. That's generally true, but a more precise statement is that people resist change when it's introduced too rapidly. If you can introduce change gradually, your people will accept it. In completely changing the rules so that it appears there's been a radical redefinition of the job, you're asking for real trouble unless the employees understand the reason for the change. They're being told to move out of their comfort zone; every habit they've formed and every bit of training they've received is being completely ignored. Most operational changes can and should be introduced gradually. In the few cases where they have to be introduced radically, perhaps overnight, you have no choice. You must then absolutely and thoroughly explain the necessity for the change.

Managing Change

All of us make changes in our work habits and in our personality, but they're so gradual that we never recognize them as change. Take a woman who worked on a particular job ten years ago; bring her back to the workplace today; she'll be amazed by the changes that have occurred in the job. A fellow worker who has remained on the job throughout those years, however, will be virtually unaware of the changes—*if* they were all introduced on a gradual basis. The more accurate statement, therefore, is that people resist uncomfortable change. Make the change comfortable for them by introducing it in small increments, and they won't fight you as severely.

What people say about change and the attitudes they display toward it are often quite different. A lot of people say "I just love variety," but watch them on the job and it's obvious that they're most content when working in what has been described as their comfort zone. The reason for this contradiction is that it's socially acceptable to want variety in a job, whereas it's not socially acceptable to be rigid or inflexible. Thus, even people who are rigid and inflexible will seldom admit it. Similarly, society is so oriented toward maintaining good human relations that we all claim to like working with people. A lot of us in fact prefer to work alone, but we don't say so because it's not socially acceptable not to enjoy working with people.

9

Disciplining the Employee

There are obviously performance standards your area of responsibility must meet. These may vary by different companies, by the nature of the work, and even by departments. They may also vary within a department. The important point as it affects discipline is that all employees must know what standards they're expected to comply with. You create nasty problems for yourself in trying to discipline an employee on the basis of nebulous work standards.

Let's assume you've done a satisfactory job of establishing standards for each job. In all probability those standards are written into a job description. The job description indicates the elements of accountability that apply to the job; you can therefore measure the individual against those standards. Now you must have methods within your area of responsibility that allow you to be constantly aware of how people are performing in relationship to the standards. You can't operate on the assumption that unless you're hearing complaints from customers, or other departments, the performance is acceptable. By the time such warning signals arrive, severe damage may already have been done.

Prior Knowledge

Your own attitude about performance is crucial. The place and time for conveying your attitude about performance to employees is when they first step into the job. They need to know exactly what's expected of them. Performance standards will change. During the training period you'll accept less in the way of quality and quantity than afterward. You should have this properly backstopped during the training period so that the trainee's errors don't get beyond your own department.

Feedback is critical to proper and effective discipline. You must know as soon as possible when performance is substandard so that it can be corrected immediately. In the following discussion of discipline procedures, let's assume that you've set adequate standards and that the employee knows what those standards are. Further, you have an adequate method of feedback so that you know when substandard performance is a problem.

The Private Conference

One of the oldest rules is that employee discipline should always be done in private. Never humiliate an employee, even in cases of dismissal. (Dismissal is covered in Chapter 11.) He must always be made to understand that what is being criticized is the performance, not the person. This is one of the most difficult attitudes for a manager to convey. Many people are unable to differentiate between criticism of their work and criticism of themselves. They consider criticism of their work a personal affront. You have to work very hard at making sure they understand it has nothing to do with whether or not you like them. You must convey the idea that you have a mutual interest in bringing the substandard performance up to a satisfactory level.

Religiously avoid making statements that can be interpreted as a personal attack. Never say, "I want to talk to you about your mistake." Never say, "You made a mistake." Never say, "You're not performing well." Such statements will only result in your having to spend most of your time trying to get the employee into a positive frame of mind so you can discuss the performance of the work. Rather, approach the problem on the assumption that the employee wants to do a good job. You might say, "I know you are concerned about the quality of your work." The vast majority of the time that will be true. People want to perform well. They have nothing to gain by performing badly, unless they want to be fired.

Attack the substandard performance by viewing it as the result of some misunderstanding about how the work should be done. Perhaps the employee has missed something in the training process, and this has created a systems deficiency that's causing the work to fall below the company's standards. By taking this approach, you inform the employee from the outset that you're talking about the performance and not the person.

Give and Take

You should have a conversation, not deliver a monologue. Many managers do all of the talking, meanwhile building up resentment in the party on the receiving end. You need to encourage the employee's participation in the conversation. Without it there's a good chance you won't solve the problem.

Be careful, now, and don't go overboard! Some executives, in their effort to be scrupulously fair, become so cautious and tactful that the employee leaves their office expecting to get a raise for outstanding performance. You have to make certain that your subordinate understands that the work is not up to standards. How you say it, though, is critically important.

When bringing the employee into your office, put him or her at ease. This may not seem like a big thing to you, but to an employee who doesn't often enter the sanctum of the high and mighty, you're the boss and being called into your presence may be a frightening prospect. Therefore, do everything you can to make the other comfortable.

Encourage the employee to participate in the discussion early in the game. You might start off with a statement like this: "Fred, you've been with us three months now and I think it's time we had a conversation about how you're getting along. As you know, I have a great interest in your being successful on this job. How do you feel things are going?"

By using this approach, you encourage an employee who

is not performing up to standards to bring up the subject. It seldom comes as a surprise to an employee to learn that specified standards are not being met. Surprise is likely only if the employee has never been told what is expected. If that's the case, you really have some serious problems—problems of training and communication.

As the employee describes how things are going, you direct the conversation to the standards that are not being met. For example, you ask, "Do you think you're getting close to the standards we've established for experienced employees?" If the answer is yes, you could ask, "Do you believe you're performing at the same level as an experienced employee?" If the answer is again yes, then the employee may be out of touch with reality. The point is to continue asking questions of this type until you get the kind of response that will lead you into discussion of the quality of the work.

Obviously, if all your tactful efforts have failed to induce the employee to bring up the crucial subject, then you have no choice but to insert it into the conversation yourself. To the employee who persists in asserting that things are going well, you could say, "That's an interesting observation you've made about the quality of the work, because my observation indicates that it's not up to the standards we've set for the job. Why do you suppose my information is different from yours?" You then have the matter out on the desk for discussion.

Eliminate Misunderstanding

As you proceed further into the conversation, you use techniques that ensure that the employee knows what's expected. It's a good idea to get feedback on what you've mutually agreed upon, so there can be no misunderstanding later about what was said.

One way to make certain of this is to write a memorandum at the conclusion of the conversation and place it in the employee's file. This becomes particularly important if you're managing a lot of people and it's possible that six months from now you won't remember the details of the conversation.

The Primacy of the Person

There are problems about an employee's performance that cannot be separated from the person. When talking about the quality or quantity of an employee's work, it's obvious that the techniques I've just discussed can help in establishing firmly in the employee's mind that a difference exists between your criticism of the work and your view of the person. But with certain attitudinal problems it's more difficult to make the distinction, and in many cases it can't be done.

Let's assume you have a highly satisfactory employee who can't seem to get to work on time. Disciplining unsatisfactory employees is easier than disciplining a problem employee like this one whom you obviously want to keep. What happens in such situations is that if you allow the employee the privilege of coming in late every day, you're going to create a morale problem with the rest of the people who adhere to the office hours, no matter how superior that person's performance is. (What I'm saying obviously does not apply if your office has flexible working hours.)

In talking with the satisfactory employee about this problem, one of the better approaches is to explain the management difficulties you'd have if every employee ignored the working hours. You couldn't tolerate that situation. In addition, the employee is creating difficulties for himself. You can then go into the discussion in some detail and start working on a solution. Let's follow through with this problem of the tardy employee, because it happens often enough that you'll eventually have to face it.

Most conscientious employees who are doing a satisfactory job will react positively to your statements. You may notice that for the next ten days or so they appear at their desks on time. At that point you'll be feeling pretty smug about your success in managing people. You'll find, however, that when the pressure is off, the reformed employees will be coming in late again. You can't take a casual approach about this and assume it was just an unusual set of circumstances. All your subordinates must be made to know you expect them to be on time every day.

I would recommend that the first time this happens after your initial conversation, you again have a discussion with the offender. This doesn't have to be a full-blown dialogue of the same length and detail as the first one. All you need to do is reinforce what you said previously. There may have been a sound reason for the latest tardiness, and it could be that the second conversation will keep the employee on the straight and narrow. If you can get to the point where the employee is coming to work on time for approximately six months, you may assume you've changed that person's work patterns enough so that you no longer have a serious problem. What you should expect from that point on is the same attendance as you get from the rest of your employees.

Some Personal Experiences

I had something of this kind happen to me a number of years ago. The only difference from the situation just described is that this employee's performance was only slightly better than mediocre. I couldn't in clear conscience say the man was satisfactory. He was barely good enough to avoid being fired for incompetence. It got so bad that the people who worked around him nicknamed him "Sleepy." He really didn't come alive until about 10:00 A.M. I thought his first two tardinesses might have had just cause, but I became concerned when he volunteered no reason for being late. So on the third tardiness I had a talk with him and was told that he had difficulty getting started in the mornings. I sympathized with him, since I had the same problem. Because he was repeatedly arriving ten minutes late, I suggested he set the clocks in his house forward fifteen minutes. He said he'd try this, but he found that it didn't work. I then decided on a different approach.

I asked the employee if there was any physical reason for his having trouble getting started in the morning, perhaps anemia. He said that was not the case; he just was unable to get going in the morning. He had had this trouble all his life, through school and on his previous job.

The previous job had been in a small office where being

on time was not considered critical. I then explained why it was important in the current situation, since the company employed a great number of people. In allowing one person to have a different starting time from all the rest, we created a problem as far as equitable treatment of employees was concerned. I then suggested the possibility of his going to bed earlier at night, and discovered the man was already sleeping twelve hours a night. I again told him it was very important that he solve the problem; in fact, his job depended on it.

I must admit that the situation did get better for about a week, but then the employee started slipping back into the old tardiness routine again. I need hardly add that the man had no trouble leaving on time at the end of the day. Following several further conversations with the offender, I ended by terminating him.

The situation just described is one that many executives would view as a failure of management skills. That's wrong. Not every personnel problem can be solved by accommodation. As far as I was concerned, I had done everything I could to remedy the situation, even to the point of suggesting that the employee visit his doctor for help. Since nothing I did worked, the only solution I had was to change to a new employee.

It's possible that you'll have other problems of a similar nature, such as spending too much time on coffee breaks, overstaying the lunch hour, or failing to be at the desk at a certain time. Needless to say, you don't run a sweatshop, and everyone will occasionally be tardy at some time or other. What's critical is dealing effectively with chronic offenders who create management problems for you and the organization.

Another difficult problem that you wouldn't expect in this day and age is cleanliness. This did happen to me once. The people working around the woman involved complained about the aroma emanating from her area. I avoided facing up to the problem because I was a new, young supervisor at the time and wasn't sure how to handle it. Eventually, I did face it and did have a conversation with the woman. She assured me that she bathed daily; we finally arrived at the joint conclusion that perhaps she wasn't getting her clothing dry-cleaned or washed as often as necessary to solve the problem. She did solve the problem, but left three months later, I think out of personal embarrassment.

If I had that one to handle over again, I believe I'd arrange to have someone in personnel talk directly to the employee rather than do it myself. The reason would not be to avoid a difficult situation, but rather to spare the woman embarrassment every time she saw me and the misery of being constantly reminded of the uncomfortable conversation. By having someone in personnel talk to her away from her work area, I might have solved the problem and also have been able to salvage an otherwise satisfactory employee. As it turned out, the woman moved out of town shortly after she quit, because her husband was transferred by his employer to another location, so I'd have lost her anyway.

Another situation that I recall along this line involved a man who was handling punch cards that were passed along from one area to another. I received a complaint because the man was always picking his ears and the person receiving the work from him didn't like handling soiled cards. I felt that the complaint might be legitimate; however, I decided against discussing it with the offender. Rather, I suggested to the man doing the complaining that he was perhaps being a little overly critical. I didn't say it in exactly that manner, but I let the man know that I didn't consider it quite as serious as he did. It was one of those problems that went away by itself.

This might be the place to make the observation that sometimes doing nothing is the right approach to solving a problem. But you have to be careful not to adopt a laissez-faire management attitude and assume that many problems will solve themselves.

The Disciplinary Approach

Getting to matters of greater seriousness, you might use a disciplinary approach in situations where you're attempting to correct performance. For example, you have a highly satisfactory employee whose work sharply deteriorates. Needless to say, you're continually communicating with the employee about the deterioration. You want to retain the employee, but you find that your words are not being taken seriously. In a situation like that you may recommend zero salary increase for the employee for that year, with a full explanation as to why you're doing it. Inform the employee in advance that if the work doesn't get better there'll be no increase in pay. Having made that threat or stated that possibility of action, you must then follow through on it so that you don't lose credibility. Some people don't actually believe you'll take such action. It's a technique that frequently works because people still care about the paycheck.

Another disciplinary technique you can use is to put the employee on probation. State that you have work deterioration that needs to be corrected and you want to give the employee every opportunity to correct it. You must make it perfectly clear that the substandard level of work being delivered cannot be allowed to continue. Also, you should set a deadline for a resolution to the problem. You might say to the employee, "This problem has to be solved within one month or we'll have to make other arrangements."

But first the employee must be made to understand exactly what kind of performance is being labeled substandard. The employee must also know how to correct it and must know what level of performance is expected. You mustn't arrive at the end of the probationary period only to find a legitimate difference of opinion as to how the employee is performing. The standards must be set so clearly that no disagreement about whether they've been met or not is possible. They must be measurable standards. You must keep a satisfactory set of records, because you may have to justify firing the employee if it comes to that.

Records are also helpful in raising performance standards. You can use the records to show your subordinates how they improved the quality of their work. This becomes an added gain because the employees are inspired to greater effort by pride in their accomplishment.

New employees in a company are often put on probation, either in line with standard company policy or as individual cases. You can't establish a probationary period for every employee in your department or division if it's not a company-wide practice. Many companies use a ninety-day probationary period. Employees doing satisfactory work at the end of that time are taken off the probationary rolls and become regular employees. It's also customary to give a modest salary increase in recognition of satisfactory completion of the probationary course. If the work is not satisfactory at that point, the employee should anticipate being terminated. Again, it should never come as a surprise.

The Mood Modifier

Some executives use a technique that I refer to as the *mood modifier*. This is pretty subtle, and it takes a good actor to pull it off. I'm not sure I recommend it, but you should be aware of it in case it's ever pulled on you. As the name of the technique implies, the manager modifies the mood of the conversation in dealing with an employee whose performance is not satisfactory. For example, if you're having trouble with an employee who's constantly late, you may have to seem more angry around the employee than you actually are in order to gain his or her attention. This is done to avoid direct examination of the issue. Letting an employee know you're dissatisfied by appearing to be irritated is unfair, however, because the employee may misinterpret what it is that's troubling you. The imagined inadequacy may not be the one you had in mind at all.

All of us, from time to time at the office, fall under the spell of moods that reflect outside situations that are troubling us. Many books on management tell us we must leave our problems at the door, or at home, and not bring them into the office. I think that attitude is naïve, because few people can completely shut off a personal problem and keep it from affecting how they perform on the job.

There's no doubt, however, that you can minimize the impact a problem has on your work. The first step is to admit that something is irritating you and that it may affect your relationship with your co-workers. If you can do that, you can probably avoid making others victims of your personal problem. If an outside problem is gnawing at you and you have to deal with an employee in a critical situation, I see nothing wrong with saying to the employee, "Look, I'm really not in the greatest mood today. If I seem a little irritated, I hope you'll forgive me." This kind of candor is refreshing to a subordinate.

Never think for a moment that others don't have the ability to judge your moods. By showing dramatic changes of mood, you become less effective. In addition, your subordinates will know when to expect these changes, what the telltale signs are, and they'll avoid dealing with you when you're on the bottom swing of such a mood. They'll wait until you're on the high end of the pendulum.

Managing Your Feelings

You should work hard at being even-tempered. But I don't think it's a good idea to be the kind of manager who's bothered by nothing. I'm talking about the person who never seems to feel great joy, great sorrow, great anything. People will not identify with you if they believe you disguise all your feelings.

Keeping your cool all the time is another matter. There are good reasons for keeping your cool. If you can always remain fairly calm, even in troubled situations, you're more likely to think clearly and so be in a better position to handle tough problems. But it's also important that you show feelings once in a while, or people will think you're a management robot.

To be an outstanding manager of people, you have to care about people. That doesn't mean taking a missionary or social-worker approach toward them, but if you enjoy their company and respect their feelings, you'll be much more effective in your job than the supervisor who's mostly "thing" oriented.

This, indeed, is one of the problems companies bring on themselves when they assume that the most efficient worker in an area is the one who should be promoted to management. That worker may be efficient because of being "thing" oriented. Moving such "experts" into areas where they supervise others doesn't automatically make them "people" oriented.

10

Hiring and Training New Employees

There are probably as many different hiring practices as there are companies. If I were to attempt to cover all the various methods, I'd never get to the end of this chapter, so let's make a couple of simple assumptions. Let's say the personnel department does the initial screening but you have the ultimate decision-making authority as to who comes to work in your area of responsibility.

The Use of Tests

With greater federal, state, and sometimes city participation in hiring procedures, your company may not do much testing of prospective employees. I'm aware of one company that has done away with all such tests. Instead, it uses only what I call *posthiring tests* to fire people early in the game if they don't cut the mustard.

This is the most expensive method of testing I can think of. I suspect it's an overreaction to government involvement in hiring procedures. Companies may increasingly resort to this method as their frustration levels increase. In so doing they make the problems of management more difficult, not to mention the psychological damage done to people who are fired when their only mistake was in having been hired in the first place.

The quality of prospective employees will vary a great deal. When unemployment rates are high, you'll find greater interest being shown in the job and you'll have a larger number of prospects to choose from. The reverse will be true when unemployment rates are low. I've known situations where available employees were so few that you'd consider hiring anyone who appeared at your desk. So there'll be forces beyond your control. We're concerned here with situations you can control.

If tests are used by your personnel department, consider first those that are relevant to the position to be filled. Math aptitude may not be important if you're hiring for a typing or secretarial job; ability to spell would be more to the point.

The Screening Process

The way to begin your screening is by thoroughly reviewing the job description. Some managers make the mistake of wanting the applicant to do better than average on all the tests. If you take that approach you could very well pass up a person who would do an outstanding job for you.

Your interview with the prospect is a two-way "sizing up" meeting. Naturally, the prospect wants the job, so she will feed you answers that are calculated to win your approval.

Don't ask such difficult questions that the prospect can't possibly answer them. Here are a few questions I think you should avoid:

"Why do you want to work here?"
"What makes you think you're qualified for this job?"
"Are you interested in this job because of the salary?"

Dumb questions like that will make you a rotten interviewer. You must strive to put the prospect at ease so that you can carry on a conversation. Your aim is to know the prospect as a person, and that means avoiding an eyeball-to-eyeball confrontation. Rather, you should make statements or ask questions that will relax the interviewee. If you have to ask a difficult question, wait until the other is at ease, so it doesn't seem so tough. A sample interview with a hypothetical applicant by the name of Mrs. Valencia follows.

Mrs. Valencia's Job Interview

"I see by your application, Mrs. Valencia, that one of your hobbies is oil painting. I used to do a little oil painting myself. How did you get started with oil painting as a hobby?"

A question like that accomplishes several things. The two of you have something in common. You get Mrs. Valencia talking about herself and her interests. You let her know you're sincerely concerned about her apart from the job. You're interested in her as a person. It's important that you develop that kind of relationship. If this woman is going to work for you, it's the beginning of what could be years of daily contact. And even if she doesn't get the job, she'll feel kindly toward you and your company because you've shown a sincere interest in her.

It's a good idea to spend several minutes talking about the prospect's personal interests before getting around to discussing the job itself. When that time does at last come—and assuming the prospect indeed has a chance for the job—you might consider this approach:

"Mrs. Valencia, before we start talking specifically about the position you've applied for, I'd like to tell you a little about our company. Because, while we're considering you, you're also considering us, so we want to answer any questions you may have about our company." Then go ahead and tell her something about the company. Tell her what your purpose is, but don't spend a lot of time on statistics. Talk more about the company's relationship with its employees. Tell her anything in this area that's unique. You want her to get a feel for the company and its people.

What you're trying to determine is how this prospect's attitudes measure up to what you expect of the person you want in the position.

During the course of this conversation you should be able to determine attitudes. Does the prospect ask questions about the work, the opportunities for promotion, the educational opportunities the company makes available? Or do the questions follow a narrower path: What are the hours? How much vacation do I get? How much sick leave do I get each month?

All these questions may come up during the course of the interview, but what the prospect asks first may give you some clue about her attitude. Be careful not to trigger the order of the questions, however. During the interview you'll eventually answer all her questions. The idea is to leave the discussion freewheeling enough early in the interview so that the prospect's questions will give you some clue as to what her attitudes are.

You must put the questions in the proper perspective. If the first question asked is about the work schedule and you know the applicant has school-age children, she may be thinking of what she needs in the way of child care. In that case, if the next questions have to do with the work, or with promotional possibilities, then you probably aren't dealing with a person who's concerned only about benefits.

That doesn't mean benefits aren't important. They are important. But if you employ people who seem concerned only about what they're going to receive and not at all about what they can contribute or people who aren't particularly interested in knowing whether the job will be challenging or not, it will show up in their performance.

The Effects of Unemployment Rates

Again concerning unemployment rates, if your town has a high unemployment rate, you'll get better acting performances from prospective employees. (If you desperately needed steady work and a steady paycheck, you'd take almost any kind of job. You'd also be more adroit in selling the interviewer on why you should have the job.)

With high unemployment rates, you'll also run into over-qualified applicants. Frankly, I have mixed emotions about these people. I strongly empathize with them in their current difficulty, but I also realize that once opportunities open up that make it possible for them to cash in on their qualifications, you lose them.

If you can anticipate that opportunities will open up in your company that may suit the overqualified person, you may be able to retain him or her. I don't know how you can forecast such a situation. If the prospect is desperate for a job, he or she may be completely honest in expressing an intention to stay at the post on a long-term basis. But if the prospect is a trained engineer working at a clerical position, he will have a tough time feeling an obligation to the company when a job comes up elsewhere that allows him to return to the engineering profession.

So if you do decide to hire overqualified people, plan on losing them. It's that simple, unless the employees are what are called *comfort-zone underachievers*.

The Comfort-Zone Underachiever

A comfort-zone underachiever (CZU) is a person who is highly qualified but doesn't like being challenged. There are a lot of them around, but very few of them admit it.

One of the main problems for CZUs is convincing you they genuinely want to work at a position that seems far below their capacity. They often get burned, in that they're not hired for jobs they want because they're overqualified. They soon discover that the way to handle this is not to list all their qualifications on the job application. The registered nurse who doesn't want to practice nursing may not indicate her training in that field. She may trim her list of qualifications to fit the clerical job she wants. Likewise, the schoolteacher who really can't stand young children in a classroom environment may not list all his credentials. Handling previous work experience on the job application gets more difficult because the trained interviewer will zero in on any gaps. So if our teacher really wants the job as the office "lawn man," his application might show him as a member of the school's "maintenance crew" rather than of its teaching staff.

Since you're interested in getting ahead and managing other people, you may have trouble understanding applicants with this kind of personality. Don't underestimate them. They certainly aren't stupid. They see work from a different perspective than you do. It isn't a matter of who's right and who's wrong. Each attitude is right for the people involved.

It's like the forty-five-year-old CZU dentist who despised the nineteen-year-old he once was because of the decision to spend the rest of his life looking into mouths and filling teeth. There are a lot of unhappy people working at unsuitable jobs and we should respect CZUs for having the courage to change their situation. People resist change, and the combination of resisting change and knowing change is necessary leads to inner emotional conflict. I believe that's what psychologists call avoidance—avoidance conflict: You're trapped by having to choose between two unpleasant alternatives, because by doing nothing you're eating yourself alive.

The comfort-zone underachiever is trying to find "what's right for me." The job CZUs take may be temporary; they're at a crossroads in a period of reassessment. Often they're looking for a job that won't divert them from their search. The job will require a minimum of attention, thus freeing them to think, to sort things out. Often they'll go after a job that's highly repetitive in nature, that can be done accurately without effort, thus enabling them to daydream. Certain jobs in your own company would doubtless drive you bananas in two hours, but there are people who enjoy doing those jobs; it's a matter of the proper fit.

Work and Play

The word *work* has a bad image for many people. To them, work is a form of punishment. Perhaps it goes back to the ejection of Adam and Eve from the Garden of Eden. If they had not been driven out, they'd still have had to figure out a way to occupy themselves, but the activities would have been by choice and so would have been thought of as play rather than as work. If I play tennis for a living (in which case I'd starve to death), it's work; but if I play it for recreation, it's play. It's still tennis. Perhaps it comes down to a distinction between have-to and want-to situations. That's why many people who are independently wealthy still work. For them it's a want-to situation.

Describing the Job

Let's get back to your interview with your prospective employee, Mrs. Valencia. In talking with her about the job, describe it in nontechnical terms. Use terms that her experience indicates she'll understand. Every business seems to develop a jargon or shorthand that all the experienced employees understand. It may have become so automatic a part of your own vocabulary that you'll have to make a conscious effort to avoid using it. Such jargon is often threatening to a new employee.

It's because of this mumbo jumbo that I have mixed emotions about showing the applicant the job description. If it's written in all this office jargon, it might be better to wait until the new employee is on the job a while.

Making the Hire

If you're considering several people for the job, be careful not to mislead any of the prospects. Tell them plainly that several people are being considered. Tell them that only after all the prospects have been interviewed will you make the selection. Never leave them feeling bitter by implying, "Don't call us, we'll call you." Tell them when the decision will be made. Then see that they're phoned on that day and informed of the decision.

There are many methods for communicating with people. I prefer that all the prospects be phoned by the personnel department and told that a decision has been made. You might of course want to deliver the good news yourself and phone the person selected. This approach may make you a big shot with Mrs. Valencia, but it won't do a whole lot for your image among people in the personnel department. They handle the dirty work; you handle the good news. If they have to inform nine people that they didn't get the job, the least you can do is let them also bring the good news to the tenth.

The Attitude Talk

After the applicant is selected for the job, you should have your "attitude talk" with the person. I'll give a summary of my own version of an attitude talk; you'll develop your own style after a while, but the basic thoughts will remain the same.

"One of the reasons you were selected for this position is that you display the kind of attitude that we consider essential. Your application and the tests you took indicate that you have the capacity to handle the position. But a lot of people can do the job. It's how they do it that's important to us. We think the difference between an outstanding employee and an average one is a matter of attitude. You'll find both kinds of people in this organization. The attitude we're talking about is one where you aren't worrying about whether or not you're doing more than your share. It's an attitude of pride in doing high-quality work. It's an attitude of accomplishment when the day is done. It's an attitude that tells you you'll benefit more if you can find satisfaction in what you do. We believe you display that kind of attitude, and coupled with your ability to handle the job, that should make you an outstanding addition to our organization."

Now let's analyze the reasons for some of the statements in that minispeech.

When is an employee most likely to be receptive to ideas about the job? I think it's on being hired and on beginning the job.

Do people generally try to live up to the image they think you have of them? I think they do.

Is it imperative to let a new employee know there are people in the organization who are intolerant in certain matters? The bad news will reach the new employee anyway, and sooner than you might expect; your candor will be refreshing.

Is it harmful to suggest to new employees that they should feel a sense of accomplishment at the end of the day? I think not. In fact, the thought might not have occurred to them at all, or as soon, if you had not suggested it.

The exact moment for having your attitude talk with a new employee is a matter of personal preference. I prefer doing it on hiring day, with reinforcement the day the employee starts on the job. This has mainly to do with the nervousness of the employee the first day on the job.

Remember your own first day with a new company. You were probably nervous and apprehensive. You worried about whether your co-workers would like you—or whether you'd like them. You worried about whether you'd catch on quickly enough to the instructions you were given. You worried about looking stupid.

Your Attitude Toward Training

Many new managers believe they must know how to perform every job in their area of responsibility. It's as though they feel that if some key person quits, they might have to get out there and personally perform the task. If you believe in that philosophy and carry it to its logical conclusion, then the chief executive officer of the organization ought to be able to perform every job in the company. That of course is ridiculous. It's just as ridiculous as believing that the President of the United States should be able to perform every task in the federal government. The President shouldn't even be able to perform every job in the White House. You don't have to be a master chef to recognize rotten chicken.

You need to know what needs to be done, not exactly how it's done. A lot depends on what level manager you are. If you are what I call a performer-manager, you are responsible for doing some of the work yourself and leading others in the same function. In that set of circumstances you will know how to perform the operation.

However, if you have thirty-five people performing a variety of tasks, you will not know how to perform each task—but you will have someone out there (in addition to the basic operator) who does know how it's done. The administrator of a large hospital is not able to perform surgery, but that administrator knows the process by which skilled surgeons are secured and retained on the staff.

Many new managers are uncomfortable about what they can't do. Don't be. You're going to be held responsible for the results you achieve within the confines of company policy. You will not be responsible for crossing every *t* and dotting every *i* yourself.

Although this concept may be frightening to you at first, you'll get used to it and wonder how you could have ever thought otherwise. Your initial reaction will be, "I've got to know it all." If it's a big, varied operation, you can't possibly know it all. Don't sweat it.

Training the New Employee

In many ways, instructions given employees on their first day are wasted motion. Their first day on the job is an opportunity for new employees to get acquainted with the people they'll be working with and to find out where the rest rooms are. You should permit them to spend the first day just observing and then start the actual training the second day. Many workers go home from their first day on the job with either a bad headache or a backache—undoubtedly the result of nervous tension.

There are different philosophies on how a person should be trained. The most common philosophy holds that a new employee should be trained by the person leaving the job. Automatically following that philosophy can be a mistake. Everything depends on why the employee is leaving and on her attitude.

The Wrong Way: An Example

Let me give an example of the wrong way to train a new employee. It demonstrates the worst kind of judgment I've ever seen displayed in this type of situation. The manager of an office consisting of several salespeople and one clerical person decided that the clerk should be fired for incompetence. He gave her two weeks' notice but asked her to work during that time. He then hired her replacement and asked her to train the new employee. The result was a nightmare for all concerned.

And no wonder! If the person leaving your company is less than 100 percent competent, you must never allow him to do the training. Most people who put in their notice don't "give a damn" from that point on. The training they do will be casual and incomplete. In addition, they may pass all their bad habits on to the new employee. On the other hand, when a position opens up because the incumbent in the job is being promoted, that person is probably the best one to handle the training.

Concerning the manager who wanted the fired employee to train the replacement, he did not himself understand the clerical job. It was impossible for him personally to train the new employee—any attempt to do so would merely have displayed his ignorance. He therefore went to impossible extremes to "keep his cover." That's a serious managerial failure.

But don't misconstrue what I've said to mean that a manager must personally know how to perform every job in the organization. I don't mean that at all. In the example given, however, there was only one clerical operation. If the manager didn't know that elementary job, how in the world could he effectively manage? The answer is he couldn't!

Managing the Small Office

I've known of situations in small offices with a single secretary and a couple of clerks where the manager takes the attitude "You handle all of the office routine and the paperwork. I don't care how you do it as long as you get the job done and as long as you can find what I'm looking for."

I don't see how you can manage a small office that way. How do you measure the performance of your subordinate? What is your standard of measurement? Too often people told to do it their own way set out to make themselves indispensable and succeed in the effort.

Unfortunately, that kind of situation prevails in far too many small offices. The clerical staff becomes the office manager and develops systems no one else can figure out. That must not be allowed to occur. The executive in a small office must understand the systems and must forbid any system to develop that enhances the indispensability of subordinates. The system must be the company's and not the employees'.

A Solution: The Work Manual

Some companies solve this problem by putting together a work or desk manual that describes the basic office duties and how they're to be performed. Routine clerical positions lend themselves better to this treatment than more complicated tasks do. Jobs requiring judgment cannot easily be reduced to simple written instructions because all their contingencies cannot be anticipated.

Work manuals are fine if they're kept current. If they're not, they become worthless.

The Role of the Trainer

Before starting a new employee on a training course, you should have a talk with the prospective trainer. You should never spring it as a surprise, so that the first time the trainer learns of the assignment is when you appear on the scene with the new employee in hand. The discussion should take place far enough in advance to permit the trainer to arrange her schedule so that the added workload can be accommodated. That may mean reassigning office duties for the duration of the training period.

You must outline to the trainer what you want to happen. If you'd like the first day to be casual, the trainer has to know how you want it handled.

You must continue to display interest in the new employee. Sometime during the latter part of the first day, you should stop by and ask the trainer and the trainee how things are going. What you say isn't important. Your display of interest is what's important.

Another step I recommend is a follow-up talk near the end of the new employee's first week on the job. I'd make this a more formal conversation. I'd call the employee into my office. Again, what is said is not as important as the interest displayed in the new employee's welfare.

A couple of questions, however, should be asked. You should find out if the instructions from the trainer are clear. You should also find out if the new employee is starting to get a handle on the purpose of the job.

The Improvement Seed

This is also the time for planting the *improvement seed*. The process might take the form of this discussion with the employee:

"As a new person on this job you bring fresh insights to the position that the rest of us may not have. After you've been at it a while, you may not be able to see the forest for the trees. I encourage you to ask any questions about what we do and why we do it. After you've been trained, we encourage you to offer any suggestions you can think of to improve what we're doing. Just because you're new doesn't mean your ideas are invalid. What seems obvious to you as a new employee may not be so obvious to the rest of us."

The reason for emphasizing "after you've been at it" is to keep new employees from suggesting changes before they understand what's going on. What may seem like a good idea early in the training may be taken care of as the nature of the position becomes more clearly understood.

Everyone you manage must know that you regularly do this improvement number. In that way you make it less likely that they'll react negatively to new ideas.

You'll always have plenty of problems with people who defend themselves with the statement "We've always done it this way." Such an argument is usually desperate; it tells you unmistakably that the person using it can't come up with a valid explanation of why something is being done.

The Job Defined

During the training period, it's a good idea to break the job down into small parts and teach the functions one at a time. In showing new employees the entire function, you run the risk of overwhelming them. You should, of course, explain the purpose of the job first.

Feedback

It's important to develop a method of feedback that lets you know how well the trainee is doing after beginning to work unassisted on the job. The trainee should take over the job from the trainer on a gradual basis as each step in the process is mastered. The feedback method should apply to every employee. The system should be developed in such a manner that unsatisfactory performance always comes to your attention before too much damage is done. The process is vital to your success as a manager, but no strict guidelines can be offered for establishing it because it will vary according to the line of business you're in.

The feedback must be internal. Hearing about the mistake from a dissatisfied client or customer means it's already too late. You want to correct the problem before the work gets out of your own area of responsibility.

Quality Control

If it's possible to maintain quality control procedures your employees can relate to, so much the better. Don't expect perfection; that's an unrealistic goal. Determine what an acceptable margin of error should be for your area and then strive as a team to reach that goal and eventually better it. The goal must be realistic if you expect the cooperation of your staff.

A baseball player batting .250 can make out extremely well in the major leagues. One batting .300—getting the job done three times out of ten—is now considered a superstar. You can't survive with that kind of percentage. Depending on what kind of business you're in, it's questionable that you could survive even with a 10 percent rate of error. Let's use a 5 percent rate of error for discussion purposes, even though it may not be realistic for your business.

New employees need to know what's expected of them once they're operating on the job alone. If your ultimate goal for them is 95 percent efficiency, it would help them if they knew what your interim targets are. You might expect them to be working at 70 percent efficiency at the end of thirty days, at 80 percent efficiency at the end of sixty days, and at 95 percent efficiency at the end of ninety days. This will depend on how difficult the work is. The simpler the job, the easier it should be to get to the ultimate quality goal. You have to determine ths timetable and let the new employee know what it is.

Even when the new employees take over the job on their own, you should have the trainer audit their work until you believe the work is acceptable and quality checks are not so crucial.

Each mistake should be gone over carefully with the trainee. The trainer should explain what was done wrong, what should have been done, and the reasons. Correcting mistakes as close as possible to the time of performance is helpful, because the trainee can probably remember why something was done that particular way. Every once in a while a mistake will be made that the trainee can't explain. In that case there's nothing to be gained by pressing the matter.

End of the Training Period

A final statement should be made about the training process. At some point the probationary period must end. In most companies this is usually after a specified number of weeks or months. However, I believe that once the trainee demonstrates the ability to work unassisted, it's time for another formal interview between you and the trainee. This marks the completion of a phase in the new employee's career, and some attention should be paid to the event. All you really need do is express your satisfaction about the progress made up to this point, note that the employee will now be working on his or her own, and indicate how the work will be monitored both for quality and for quantity.

11

"Oh My God, I Can't Fire Anyone!"

If there's one moment that will live forever in a manager's memory, it's the first time a subordinate has to be fired. It's not a pleasant task. If you enjoy it, then I question your ability to manage people.

Firing someone can be traumatic for both parties in the drama. If you've done your job properly, the event will not come as a surprise to the person who is about to get the ax.

Sudden firings are nearly always wrong, except in cases where an employee has been dishonest or violent. Never fire someone when you're angry. Never take such radical action on an impulse. When a subordinate pushes you over the edge and you feel like "showing who's boss," don't give in to your emotions. If you do, you'll regret it.

As you read this chapter, the thought may occur to you that some people don't deserve the time and consideration I'm recommending. You may be right, but I believe in erring on the side of excess deliberation rather than on the side of excess haste. In fact, some managerial friends of mine adopt the philosophy of never firing a subordinate until everyone in the office is wondering why they haven't taken the step already.

Preparing the Ground for the Divorce

Documentation of the troublesome employee's performance is critically important. Of course, you must keep such records for all your employees. If your company has a formal performance appraisal system, then you may be adequately covered.

Records are important because being sued for dismissing an employee is becoming more common. You should ask yourself, "If I have to, can I fully justify this dismissal?" If you can answer yes, that's all you need worry about.

Many supervisors agonize over every situation where they've had to let someone go. I prefer that a supervisor care too much than be completely callous about it.

Most of the firing situations don't develop overnight. Perhaps I've been extremely fortunate in my managerial life, but I've never had to fire anyone for getting into a fight and smacking someone in the mouth. That kind of situation, along with committing an office crime like stealing, clearly doesn't lend itself to my concept of "no surprise firings." Such situations are no doubt covered by company policy.

The more typical kinds of discharge that you're likely to run into in your managerial career have to do with poor performance and the employee's inability or unwillingness to abide by the company's standards. Some people will never be able to cut the job. They may get to a satisfactory training performance level but will never advance beyond that point to the performance level the job requires.

Firing is not the first thought that should come into your head. You must first satisfy yourself that the training has been correct and clearly understood. Was there any kind of personality barrier between the trainer and the trainee that impeded the flow of adequate information? Go back over the employee's aptitude tests, job application, and other initial hiring data on the chance that you may have missed something. Only after you're completely convinced that you have a below-satisfactory performer with little or no hope of bringing the performance up to proper standards should you consider termination as a possible solution.

Has the new employee been told that his or her performance is not up to the standard that is expected? You owe it to your people to let them know what the situation is. And that includes telling them when they're performing well. Too many managers assume that if employees don't get bad performance reports, they know they're doing okay. I've got news for you. Those employees believe you "don't give a damn"—and I think they're right on target.

Mergers and Buy-Outs

Since the mid-1970s, we have been seeing an onslaught of mergers and buy-outs. Usually, everyone is told that the new corporation is planning on no personnel changes, but within six months the personnel changes begin. A reorganization takes place and some people are fired. After a corporate take-over everyone is scrambling to protect his or her own position. Some people survive and some don't. Those who do not survive are not necessarily inadequate. They may be filling positions that are duplicated in the parent organization. Some people are fired because they are too high in the organization or because their salary is too high.

If you get involved in one of these takeovers, you can only hope that the parent corporation is humane. If it is necessary to let some people go, it should be done in a way that acknowledges responsibility to these human beings. Continuing their salary for a reasonable length of time, providing office space and secretarial help while they look for a new position, and personal counseling are some methods used to soften the blow.

It is doubtful that you as manager will have anything new to tell employees about the takeover. You may get saddled with the job of telling some people in your area that they are being let go. It may even be possible that you have to select the people who are to be let go. You may have been told to reduce staff by 10 percent or reduce salary costs by 20 percent. These are difficult decisions because they often have little to do with performance. All you can do is carry out the task in as humane a manner as possible. Everyone knows the staff reduction is a result of the merger, so you might as well tie it to that; it at least allows people to save face. If they can't save their job, saving face is some consolation. Use whatever influence you have with the organization to generate some help for these people.

I have never been a great believer in seniority—countless

sins are committed in the name of "time in grade"—but if the last people hired are the first fired, at least none of them can complain that such a system is personal.

A False Sense of Superiority

This may be the right place to suggest that too many executives believe they're more intelligent than the people working for them. That may not be true. If you have the attitude that subordinate is a synonym for inferior, you're not ready for management, in my opinion. Unfortunately, business is populated with executives who feel that way, and the quality of their leadership suffers constantly from it. I don't know how you get managers with that attitude to change; perhaps the experience of a few failures is the only way.

Some executives feel they have to be smarter than all their subordinates. It'll never work. The successful executive is willing to hire people who are more competent in certain areas than she is. They'll actually make your job easier and help prepare you for additional promotion.

A Second Chance

When an employee's job performance is unsatisfactory, it is important to make clear in your discussion with the employee that you're addressing yourself to the work and not to the person. At some point in the conversation you let the employee know that termination will come if the performance standards cannot be met. But it's not enough to let it go at that. Set a target for the employee to reach, in terms of both work improvement and time to achieve the goal. You have to be specific. "You're now averaging ten errors each day. You'll have to cut this down to three errors each day by the end of two weeks." Your precise specifications serve a dual purpose. If the employee meets the goal, you may be on the way to solving the problem *and* retaining the employee. Failing that, you're ready to start the termination process.

Is it possible that this employee could handle some other job in your own area that is currently available? Or if an opening is coming up in accounting, can the employee make a contribution? Is this a situation where a person has been hired for the wrong job? Does the company gain anything by firing someone who might be useful somewhere else? Will the employee be so embarrassed by what appears to be failure that the stigma will carry over into future jobs? Is your company large enough that the employee could be moved to another area with no stigma? Former employees are part of a company's public. Can you handle the situation in such a way that you don't deplete your company's storehouse of civic goodwill? Even though the employee won't like being fired, can you handle the procedure so that the employee will admit to having been given every opportunity and will consequently agree that you had no choice in the matter?

Right here let me warn against taking the coward's way out and blaming the mysterious *they*. "As far as I'm concerned, ten errors a day isn't too bad, but *they* say we have to get it down to three, or *they* will force me to let you go." That indicates you're merely a puppet. Someone else is pulling the strings. You don't have a mind of your own.

You have to level with the employee who is not measuring up. I know of managers who sugarcoat all bad news to such an extent that the employee on the receiving end feels complimented on having done a clearly outstanding job.

Flexibility and Consistency

Some of your people will also need to be dismissed because of poor attendance. Companies have such a wide variety of sick-leave programs, however, that it's impossible to discuss what level of absenteeism is satisfactory. I personally don't care for sick-leave programs that allow, for example, one sick day per month or twelve per year, cumulatively. I prefer a method that allows supervisory discretion based on the individual situation. For example, I can decide not to dock a good, loyal employee for a day's absence. I can also decide that an employee with a bad attendance record has abused the privilege and must consequently be docked for a day's absence.

Admittedly, this kind of program is more difficult to administer than one with hard-and-fast rules to follow. In evaluating the merits of each case, you have to be able to defend your decision.

One disadvantage in having no formal program is the serious risk that decisions will not be made consistently throughout the company. Generous executives may be inclined to excuse almost any absence and pay the absentee; other managers may be more strict and dock for days missed. Having no formal program means the communication between departments and executives has to be extremely good, ensuring that approximately the same standards apply throughout the company.

The Dismissal Drama

So far we've discussed events leading up to a dismissal. Now let's talk about the dismissal itself. I'm referring to a dismissal whose timing you control.

My preference has always been to stage the drama on late Friday afternoon. By the time it's over, all the co-workers of the person being fired have left the office. Thus, the dismissed employee won't have to endure the humiliation of "clearing out" in front of an audience. Also, the employee can use the weekend to pull things together and prepare for seeking other employment, applying for unemployment compensation, or doing whatever else has to be done.

Any money due at the time of the dismissal should be given to the dismissed employee at the end of the interview. Being canned is enough of an emotional blow; wondering when the final check will arrive can only add to the misery. Severance pay—if that's the company's policy—should be given at the same time. Unused vacation time or sick leave should also be included in the compensation.

Put yourself in the other's position. You're not going to feel the termination was completely justified. Unless you receive every dollar you have coming to you, you'll probably think, "Well, I suppose I'll have to hire an attorney to get the money this chicken outfit owes me!" Remove that thought from the dismissed employee's mind by taking care of all those matters in advance.

Another courtesy that I think you owe the employee is to keep your intention to fire him or her as confidential as possible. Of course, the personnel and the payroll departments will have to know. But other than discussing it with the necessary management people, you should treat the matter confidentially.

The final scene in the dismissal drama is bound to be most uncomfortable for the supervisor. Because in that highly charged interview it's just the two of you face-to-face, and you want to get it over with as quickly as possible.

A good way to start is to review in brief what has happened. Don't drag it out and make it a recitation of all the other's mistakes. I prefer something like this: "As you know from our past conversations, we had certain standards on the job that had to be met. I think we approached reaching those standards on a fair and reasonable basis. As I've mentioned to you from time to time over the past few weeks, you haven't been able to meet those standards. I don't believe it's because of any lack of effort on your part. However, it hasn't worked out, and I don't think that comes as any surprise to you. We're going to have to terminate your services as of today. I really regret that. I wanted it to work out just as much as you did. But it hasn't worked out, and so we have to face up to reality. Here's the final check, including one month's severance pay plus your unused vacation and sick-leave time. This should give you a continuation of income for a time sufficient for you to find another job."

You can vary your remarks to fit the individual situation, but I think the above words say what needs to be said. They don't sugarcoat the bad news; I don't think they're too blunt either. You have to come up with a statement that fits the situation, and one you're comfortable with.

I assume there are no more companies that fire people by putting a pink slip in their pay envelope. That's inhumane, in my opinion. I can understand the necessity for it in a factory where thousands of people are all being temporarily laid off. I can also understand using the method if the entire business is being closed and everybody is going. Situations like that are not related to the performance of the individual. When someone is being let go because of a failure to perform or live up to company standards, the only way to handle it is on a one-on-one basis. The manager might prefer to avoid the direct confrontation, but it's part of the job's responsibilities and must be dealt with straight on.

When you consider it thoughtfully, you realize that keeping an unsatisfactory employee on the job is unfair not only to the company but also to the employee. No one is comfortable in a job he is not performing well.

I recall a situation a number of years ago where being canned turned out to be the biggest favor ever done for that young man. He was trying to function in an accounting position but was not cutting the mustard. After being let go, he decided to continue his education. He entered a law college and is now practicing his profession very successfully.

I find that people avoid the word *fire* as they do the word *die*. Instead of *die*, they say *pass away, go on to his reward*, or *cross over*. Instead of *fire*, they say *dismiss, discharge, let go, can*.

One last thought: You must be absolutely certain in your own mind that the firing is deserved. You must be sure you're being as objective as you can possibly be. If in doubt, use a more experienced executive as a sounding board. Then when you know you have to fire the employee, make sure it doesn't come as a surprise. And handle it in a considerate, humane, and delicate manner.

Three
The Manager as Administrator and Counselor

12

Your Relationship With the Personnel Department

The popular name at present for the personnel function is *human resources.* To me the term sounds as if personnel officers were in the mining business, but I'm afraid it's here to stay for a while. The broadening of the title comes about, I suspect, because in many organizations this department is also responsible for training and education. The employee assistance program is often coordinated by this department.

Please indulge me as I continue to refer to this function as the personnel department.

How much you interact with your company's personnel department will depend on how much latitude you're allowed in the selection process. In many companies the personnel department does the initial screening of prospective employees, but the final decision on hiring is left to the appropriate manager.

It's my belief that the overall selection process is strengthened if the final choice is made at the operating level. If a manager had nothing to say about the person hired and is unhappy with the choice, the new employee won't have the same chance for being successful. Fortunately, most companies do allow the operating department to make the final selection from several qualified candidates.

Although people working in personnel consider themselves experts on selecting employees, it doesn't matter who they think is the best qualified if the person is someone you don't want. How you react to the recommendations of personnel people is important. You must take their recommendations seriously. This assumes that through talks with you they fully understand what the job requires. If they don't, it's because you haven't given them the information they need. They can't be experts on every job in the company, even with access to all the job descriptions. You're the expert on the jobs in your area of responsibility, and you ought to know what's required.

You'll also become involved with the personnel department in promotions. Most of the time you'll try to promote employees from your own area; but when you have to look to other areas of the company for the staff you need, the people in personnel will be in a position to help you. For example, they can show you the original data collected when the person was hired, including scores from aptitude tests given at the time. In most cases, they'll consult with the department that employs your potential promotee and get important information you might not have gotten on your own.

Also, in some companies the personnel department administers employee benefit programs, so you could be going to personnel on behalf of subordinates who are having difficulties with some aspect of the program.

If you haven't managed people before, personnel can be a strong resource for you. You can usually go there for advice and counsel on supervisory problems you've never encountered before. The personnel department is also the usual repository for books on the management of people.

In many companies, the personnel department handles the education and training of managers. Since this department serves the entire company, you can often talk with someone there about "people problems" that you might be reluctant to discuss with your own superior. So you can look to personnel for assistance not only in selecting people but also in managing them.

I know of organizations that use the personnel department as a place where employees can go with any problems they don't wish to discuss with their own boss. This can be a valuable service both to the employees and to the company. It is hoped that your personnel department has been properly trained and educated in its function.

One or two visits to the chief of the personnel department should give you an indication of what help you can expect. You ought to cultivate a strong working relationship with everyone in the department.

13

Personal and Organizational Loyalty

Some people believe a manager must earn the loyalty of the individuals she supervises. I can't quarrel with that statement; however, it creates a problem for the first-time manager: What happens until such time as that loyalty is earned?

I suspect that most subordinates give their loyalty, albeit a bit tentatively at first, to a new manager until the manager demonstrates that she either does or doesn't deserve unreserved loyalty.

Before you conclude that loyalty flows in only one direction, let me assure you that the manager must also be loyal to the people supervised. The staff and the manager must earn each other's loyalty, with the presumption that loyalty will be deserved and warranted until the contrary is either obvious or proved.

Loyalty Is Out of Fashion

Unfortunately, loyalty in business is not a trait in vogue. There is an increasing tendency for people to feel loyal to their profession, or even to professional associations or groups, but not to the company that issues the payroll check. I won't dwell on this tendency, but I would like to share some assumptions about how the current attitude developed.

One is that, during previous periods of full employment and high demand for quality professionals, competition was high. Recruiting didn't stop at the university and college placement office. People were recruited a second, third, and sometimes even a fourth time. Keeping a job in a period of full employment was not too important, because there were always more jobs than quality people to fill them. If nothing suitable opened up from within as soon as they thought it should, these professionals simply moved on to a company that offered the position they felt they deserved—and at a considerably higher salary. It was only when an oversupply of such people began to come out of colleges and universities that job jumping ultimately slowed down.

Another factor that has hurt loyalty to the organization is the tendency of companies to bring in people from the outside. My theory, completely unproved, on why this is happening is that the shortcomings of people already within an organization are known, but those of a new person are not. He has shortcomings too, but since they are not apparent, they're not a factor in the selection process. By the time the company learns what they are, it's too late. To avoid having the hiring decision look like a mistake, the company convinces itself that a sound selection was made.

A third factor is the fear associated with mergers, downsizing, and acquisitions. People have been burned; they were loyal to owners and management, only to be sold off along with the furniture, the inventory, and the "goodwill." A merger or acquisition is not unlike the transfer of chattel or the sale of a baseball team to the highest bidder. Is it any wonder that employees get nervous when a company is acquired and new management says, "We plan no personnel cutbacks. We'll take care of any reduction in staff through attrition"?

Going to work for a company does not mean that you're sentenced to staying there the rest of your natural life. But while you're there, the company deserves your loyalty until such time as it proves itself undeserving.

Loyalty is a commendable human trait. You can't withhold it just because some day it might not be recognized, appreciated, or reciprocated. That would be like doing away with honesty because some day someone might cheat you. Good characteristics are their own reward.

Loyalty to Your Boss

What does it mean to be loyal to your boss? It means that you don't knock him to your associates. It means that you are not two-faced in the relationship, all sweetness and light to his face, then sticking pins when discussing him with office friends.

Sometimes you are put to the test. You may have an occasional rough day with the boss. However, you have your bad days too, and you'd appreciate your boss overlooking such rare occasions.

It's tempting to tell all when you've had a disagreement with your boss. But if you blast her to your friends at coffee break, you may not be able to repair the damage tomorrow when you're no longer upset. You simply can't take back the unpleasant things you say. It's the same as when a newspaper prints a retraction of an incorrect story; the people who read the original seldom see the retraction. An unpleasant statement is not offset by a compliment, because the bitter aftertaste lingers, especially if you were emotional when you made it. Remember, complimentary remarks are seldom made with the same intensity as criticism.

Bad-mouthing your boss allows the more perceptive people on your staff to wonder, "What's he saying about me when I'm not present?" Still another danger is that your complaint may not be treated in confidence. If your friends or your staff quote you, your complaint may work its way back to your boss.

Loyalty extends beyond the office as well. Don't criticize your boss away from the workplace. These things have a way of backfiring.

Loyalty to Your Company

Loyalty to the organization should be completely compatible with loyalty to your boss; if not, you have a serious problem.

People who give the name of their company in an apologetic manner send out strong negative clues. People who work solely for a paycheck and feel absolutely no loyalty to anyone or anything are not professionals. But you, because you're a manager, are a professional.

I don't want to suggest that all organizations deserve your loyalty. Far from it. Some don't deserve anyone's loyalty, but I'm assuming you wouldn't work for one of them. If you know that an organization in your community exploits its employees, takes advantage of its customers, or operates barely within the law, you simply should not work for it. If you're new in town, any respectable employment placement office can tell you the reputations of major companies looking for employees.

Unless you work for one of these few questionable companies, give the organization the benefit of the doubt. Assume that it deserves your loyalty until proved otherwise; being trusting is not being naïve. On the other hand, don't be blind to its faults and make gushy remarks that no one can believe.

You can help make your company a better place to work through your own attitude. If you believe your company has great people working for it, say so. As the word spreads, other great people will be attracted to it, with a consequent upgrading of the staff.

Loyalty should be given gladly. I doubt if you'll find it mentioned in a job description, but it's one of the most indispensable traits a manager can bring to the position.

14

Job Descriptions, Performance Appraisals, and Salary Administration

Job descriptions, performance appraisals, and salary administration are valuable functions that every company performs, either formally or informally. But if the people administering them are not properly instructed in the purpose of these functions, they can be seriously mismanaged.

We have to speak of these functions from a conceptual viewpoint. Discussion of such precise details as the forms used is unfeasible because of the great variation in approaches that exists between industries and even between companies within individual industries.

Even companies without a formal program use such techniques—although often poorly. Informality is more likely to occur in smaller companies that are controlled by family members or by one or two people at the top. Such autocrats may feel they're being equitable and that all their employees are satisfied with the fair treatment they're receiving. That may indeed be the case, but the chances for it are remote. Even without a formal program, someone in charge decides which jobs are most important (job evaluation), makes a judgment on how well people are doing (performance appraisal), and decides how much each employee is going to be paid (salary administration). So even if the motto is "We're all like one happy family, and as papa I make all the decisions on the basis of what's fair," the company does have a program—with all the idiosyncratic biases of the "papa" thrown in.

Job Descriptions

Many companies use job descriptions, although they may be called something else. A list of job descriptions should not be confused with a desk manual that tells not only exactly what has to be done on the job but also exactly how to do it. A job description, rather, tells *what* is done.

Some companies may write their own job descriptions; others may rely on management consulting services. The information required for a job description will vary widely, but certain information seems common to most job descriptions. Besides telling what is done, a typical job description usually indicates what educational background is required, how much experience is needed before a trainee in the position can be called a fully trained incumbent, what the specific accountabilities of the position are, and the extent of the supervisory responsibility.

Some methods of describing jobs will require spelling out specific objectives that are both short-term and long-term. The relationship of the person in the job to other people in the organization will often be covered. For example, what position does the job report to? With what positions in the company does the job holder interact? The description may also indicate whether the job requires contact with the public, either in person or by telephone. All these factors may play an important part in evaluating the job and determining where the position fits in the overall job hierarchy.

At some point you'll have the opportunity to write a job description either for yourself or for your subordinates. Some companies allow managers to write their own job description, and others require that the description be written by the immediate supervisor of the job. I believe it's best if the descriptions are written jointly by the employee and the supervisor, so that both are in agreement as to what the job is. A great deal of mental anguish and ineffectual performance can perhaps be avoided in that way.

As to the actual writing of the description itself, it's best not to use a lot of boilerplate copy. Also, puffing up the job to make it sound impressive usually works to your disadvantage. If a scoring committee has to go through the ordeal of sifting out the facts from all the hokum, the job may end up being ranked lower than it deserves to be.

Of course, you want a job in your area—and your own job—to score as highly as possible in the organization, but the job's actual duties will have to justify the scoring. If it were possible to determine the importance of jobs by overwriting their functions, then you wouldn't have the proper relationship between jobs within the organization. The best jobs would be those that were most effectively inflated by the writer describing them. That's in no one's best interest, because no matter how good you are at puffery, there'll always be someone who's better. Stick with the facts!

Performance Appraisals

Performance appraisals can be as informal as telling someone "You've done a nice job," or as elaborate as a full-scale written report, complete with a long follow-up interview with the employee.

Clearly, all of us like to know how we're doing. One employee will say, "Working in this office is like working in the dark." Another will say, "Old Fussbudget may be tough, but you always know where you stand." It's meant as a compliment.

A formal system of performance appraisal—for example, one or two planned contacts with the employee each year for the specific purpose of discussing "how you're doing"—is preferable to the informal method, which is often equivalent to doing nothing.

Some managers are convinced that they communicate effectively with their employees and that these employees know exactly how they stand. An interview with the employees, however, will indicate that communication is one of the greatest needs they feel.

Too many executives still approach their supervisory role with the motto "If they don't hear anything, they know they're doing okay." That doesn't cut it. Top-echelon managers too often avoid discussing all performances except those that require emergency action. They feel that performance appraisals are necessary for the rank and file, but members of the executive team are above such things. The rationale is that these officials are clearly in control of the situation and of themselves and don't need to be told how they're doing. Just the opposite is true. Members of the executive team often have an even greater need to be told how their performance is viewed by their superiors.

The Appraisal Form

A formal system should be designed in such a way that it considers as many elements of the job as possible. The manager should be forced to make some judgment about each of the important factors. This means, first of all, that the executive must be knowledgeable about the job and the performance. That's why the appraisal should be done at the level closest to the job being reviewed. A manager three levels above the position in question can't handle the judgments as well as the manager in daily contact with the employee being appraised. It can be reviewed by higher-level management, but the appraisal will be more accurate when done by someone in daily contact with the job.

Here are some items that appear on a typical performance appraisal form. There may be anywhere from three to ten degrees of performance efficiency for each category, the extremes being "unsatisfactory" on the one end and "outstanding" on the other.

- Volume or production levels
- Thoroughness

- Accuracy
- Initiative or attitude
- Ability to learn
- Cooperation
- Attendance and punctuality

You can probably think of other factors applying to your own business that ought to be included. Some systems may use a numeric weighting for each of the factors, arriving at a final rating that will be given to the employee. The entire form becomes a part of the employee's personnel file. The ranking scheme might be something like this:

80 to 100 points:	Outstanding
60 to 80 points:	Commendable
50 to 60 points:	Satisfactory
40 to 50 points:	Needs improvement
Less than 40 points:	Unsatisfactory

The ranges can be narrower if your system is designed that way. Some companies may consider anything below 70 points as unsatisfactory.

The Interview

The interview with the employee about the performance appraisal becomes crucial. You should plan to hold it at a time when you'll be unhurried and not likely to be interrupted. Allow yourself as much time as is needed to cover all facets of the job. Answer all questions. Listen to everything the employee wants to say. Your willingness to hear your subordinate out may be as important as the discussion itself. Employees are so used to dealing with managers who behave as though everything is an emergency that, when given time to talk to their superior about their own dreams and aspirations, they may feel uncomfortable.

The conversation with your subordinate is so important that you should instruct your secretary to hold your telephone calls. This should include even calls from the president of the company. Of course, anyone in any organization can be interrupted for emergencies, but you should not take phone calls of a routine nature. It's quite disconcerting to be telling another about your ambitions and feelings only to have the other break the spell by taking phone calls.

We're slaves to the telephone to an extent that's difficult to understand. How many times have you been outside the door and gone rushing back into the house to answer the phone only to find it's a magazine salesman? Somehow, there's an urgency about a telephone ringing that demands response.

I once read about an elderly gentleman who had what I consider the ideal attitude toward the telephone. One evening, while he was chatting with a neighbor over his backyard fence, his telephone could be heard ringing inside his house. The man serenely disregarded the incessant summons, until his neighbor could stand it no longer and said with some irritation in his voice, "Aren't you going to get that phone?" The man replied, "No, I put that telephone in for *my* convenience." That would indeed seem the correct attitude to take toward Mr. Bell's invention.

Getting back to the performance appraisal interview, you should direct the tone of the discussion but not dominate it. You definitely have a message to convey. You want to go over each performance appraisal factor with your subordinate. You want to make known what you consider to be your subordinate's strengths on the job and what areas require some improvement. You'll seldom get disagreement on the areas you designate as strengths. But you're likely to encounter disagreement when you get around to discussing weaknesses. And this is where you have to allow employees to express their own feelings.

Do you have documentation that indicates where the employee is weak and where improvement is needed? Your case is much stronger if buttressed by hard evidence. Production or quality records are much more convincing than an executive's intuition. When you come up against the subordinate's disagreement, that difference of opinion is important and should be discussed. It's possible that you're wrong, but you won't be if the facts can be documented.

An experiment I once engaged in was a great help to me in getting my staff to understand performance appraisals. Before sitting down to make my Solomon-like judgments, I gave all the members of my staff a blank form and asked them to evaluate their own performance. We then compared their appraisals with mine; with only one exception, their ratings were lower than mine. I'm not a liberal grader, so that wasn't the reason. We were then able to discuss our views of each factor rated. They learned a great deal about performance appraisal from the experiment, but I learned a great deal more about the people I was managing.

Too many leaders will be thorough in pointing out the areas in which the employee should show improvement, but they will not go far enough. If they're going to tell the employee where job performance is not up to expectations, then they must also tell *how* it can be improved. This needs to be thought through in great detail before the interview is even held.

The Agenda

This brings us to the preparation time that I believe is essential to a successful performance appraisal interview. You should sit down and decide what points you want to cover in the conversation. You might even prepare a brief outline of what you want to discuss. It's possible that the performance appraisal form your company uses may trigger all the proper thoughts in your mind. However, you must anticipate that it will not. You'll look quite foolish if you fail to cover all the bases and have to ask the employee to come back into your office a day later to review some important point that you forgot.

I recommend that you actually make an outline of the significant items you should cover. Here are some questions you might ask as you prepare the outline:

- What areas of this employee's performance or attitude should you mention?
- What areas not covered in the performance appraisal do you need to mention?

- What are some of the items of personal interest about this employee that you should bring up?
- What questions should you ask this employee that are likely to generate some conversation and opinions about the work?
- How can you help this employee do a better job? What are the areas in which this employee will be self-motivated?
- How can you let this employee know she is important to you personally, and not just for the work performed?
- How does this employee fit into the company's future plans? Is this person promotable? What can you do to help?

I'm sure you get the idea of the kind of self-examination you should go through before beginning the session with the employee. A few minutes spent preparing for the conversation will greatly increase the success ratio of your performance appraisal interviews.

The Satisfactory Employee

Many executives prepare quite thoroughly for the interview with the problem employee. They know it might get sticky and they'd better see to it that their flanks are protected. You should be just as thorough in preparing for the interview with the satisfactory employee. Occasionally you'll be surprised by the outstanding staff member who'll turn a conversation you thought was going to be all "sweetness and light" into a real donnybrook.

As you spend more years in management you'll find that the satisfactory employee generally uses this interview to unload some of the problems that have been festering. The problems vary with the situation. Here are some examples:

"I'm not advancing fast enough."
"My salary is not fair for the work I do."
"My co-workers are not performing up to standards."

"As manager, you don't pay enough attention to subordinates who are getting the job done."
"Good performance is not appreciated or recognized."

You should welcome such input from your satisfactory employees, even though you risk hearing what you don't want to hear. Let's face it, many employees will tell you only what they think you want to hear; but a rare and precious few will be truth-tellers, and these you must listen to carefully. Don't fall into the "shoot the messenger" syndrome. Although the news a messenger brings you makes you unhappy, the fault is not with the messenger; punishing the carrier won't change the truth of the message carried. Ignorance may be bliss, but it can be fatal in a managerial career.

Of course, the information you're receiving may not exactly reflect the facts. But even though you're receiving it through the carrier's filters, that doesn't make it any less valuable. You've been around long enough to know how to sort out what's important and what's window dressing. If the satisfactory employee believes it's important enough to bring to your attention, then you ought to listen to it. Besides, this subordinate surely knows you prefer a trouble-free interview to one filled with problems, so you know the matter would not have come up unless the employee felt strongly about it.

It's possible that you may occasionally have a mischief maker on your hands, but such people are usually not your highly satisfactory employees.

An Open-Door Policy

"My door is always open." How many times have you said it yourself? It doesn't take the employees long to find out what the statement really means.

"My door is always open, as long as you don't come in here to tell me about any new problems." That's one possible meaning. "My door is always open, but don't come in to talk about money or a better job." That's another. "My door is always open, but I don't want to hear about your personal problems." Your employees know what you really mean or they soon figure it out.

Your performance appraisal interviews should encourage your subordinates to say whatever they have in mind. The more open the communication between you, the better chance that you'll have a satisfactory working relationship.

Salary Administration

It should be pretty obvious that job descriptions, performance appraisals, and salary administration all fit together in one overall plan. They're designed to provide accurate descriptions of what people do, give fair evaluations of their performance, and pay them a salary that's reasonable for their effort. All these factors must bear a proper relationship to one another and make a contribution to the organization's overall goals.

If you have a job evaluation program, you probably also have salary ranges for each position in the organization. As a manager, you work within that scale.

It makes sense to have a minimum and a maximum salary for each position. You can't allow a situation to develop in which an individual could stay on the same job for years and receive a salary out of all proportion to what the task is worth. It's important to make certain that long-term employees are aware of this situation, especially as they get close to the salary "lid" on the job. For most well-qualified people this is not a problem, because they'll usually be promoted to another job with a larger salary range. However, in your managerial career you will encounter long-term employees who remain in the same jobs. Perhaps they don't want to be promoted. Perhaps they are at their level of competence and cannot handle the next position up the ladder.

These people need to know that there is a limit to what the job is worth to the organization. You have to tell these individuals that once they are at the maximum, the only way they can receive more money is if the salary ranges are changed on all jobs. This may happen, for example, through a cost-of-living increase that raises the ranges on all jobs by 6 percent.

Should that occur, you will have a little room for awarding salary increases.

Nonetheless, long-term employees who stay in the same job for an extended period of time and who are at maximum salary level need to have continued incentive. They are capable and should be kept on the job. Many companies have solved this problem by instituting annual financial awards (such as annual, increasing cash stipends) related to years of service. This keeps financial payments out of the job evaluation system and yet rewards the faithful long-term employee.

The salary administration program for all other employees usually includes a salary recommendation within a range of pay increases, based on the kind of performance appraisal the employee has received. Since the two procedures have such an impact on each other, some companies separate the salary recommendation from the performance appraisal rating. In that way a supervisor's idea of what a salary increase ought to be is not allowed to determine the performance appraisal given. If as supervisor you make both determinations at the same time, you'll be tempted to take the answer you want and work backward to justify it. It remains difficult to separate salary consideration from the performance appraisal, but completing the procedures several weeks or months apart may help.

So let's assume your company does have salary ranges for each job and there's some limitation on what you can recommend. No doubt the salary ranges overlap. For example, a veteran employee on a lower-level job could be paid more than a newer employee on a higher-level job. Or an outstanding performer at one level could be paid more than a mediocre worker one level up.

Equity

As the manager, you're concerned with equity. You should review the salaries of all the people who report to you. You might begin by listing all the jobs in your department, from top to bottom. You might then write the monthly salary next to each name. Based on what you know about the job performances, do the salaries look reasonable? Is there any salary that looks out of line?

Another method you can use is to rank the jobs in the order of importance to the department, as you perceive the situation. How does that compare with top management's evaluation of the importance of the jobs? If there are differences you can't reconcile or accept, then you'd better schedule a session with your immediate superior to see what can be done about it.

In this matter of rankings, appraisals, and salaries, a word of caution is in order. Recognize, and be willing to admit to yourself, that you like some employees more than others. You're conning yourself if you think you like them all equally. Certain personality types are more agreeable to you than others. Try as honestly as you can to keep these personality preferences from unduly influencing the decisions you make about appraisals, salaries, and promotions.

In recommending salary increases for several subordinates, you'll have some tricky decisions to make. If the company makes all its salary adjustments at the same time each year, then it's fairly easy to compare one recommendation against another. You can make all your decisions at one time and see how they stack up with one another. But if salary decisions occur throughout the year—for example, if they are tied to the worker's employment anniversary—it's more difficult to have all the decisions spread out in front of you.

Although maintaining equity in this type of situation is difficult, it is possible if you keep adequate records. Retain copies of all your job descriptions, performance appraisals, and salary recommendations. Some companies encourage supervisors not to keep such records and to depend on the personnel department's records. I believe that maintaining your own set is worth the effort; you'll then have the records when you want them.

The Salary Recommendation

In making a salary recommendation, be as sure as you possibly can that it's a reasonable amount. It should be neither too low nor too high and at the same time fit within the framework of the performance the company is receiving from that person. An increase that's too high, for example, could create an "encore" problem. Anything less than the same amount offered the next time around may be considered an insult by the employee. However, an unusually large increase coming at the time of a promotion doesn't run that same encore danger, because it can be tied to a specific, nonrepeating situation. In that case, you must explain to the employee why the increase is so large and why it doesn't create a precedent for future increases.

Since a small increase can be considered an insult, you'd perhaps do better to recommend no increase at all rather than a pittance. Sometimes a small increase is a cop-out and is given because the supervisor lacks the courage to recommend no increase. But this only postpones the inevitable reckoning; I recommend confronting the situation immediately and honestly.

When considering the amount of the raise, it's essential that you not allow the employee's need to be an important factor. Before you think I'm being inhumane, consider these points. If you based salary increases on need, the employee in the most desperate state of need would be the highest paid. If that person were also the best performer, you'd have no problem. But what if the employee's performance were merely average?

The common thread that must run through salary administration is merit. Basing your salary recommendations on who has been with the company the longest, who has the greatest number of children, or whose mother is ill moves you away from your responsibilities as a salary administrator and puts you in the charity business. If you have subordinates with financial problems, you can be helpful as a friend, a good listener, or a source of information about where to go for professional assistance, but you can't use the salary dollars you're charged with as a method of solving the social problems of your subordinates.

When you're making a salary adjustment for a subordinate who's having difficulty, there's a great temptation to add a few more dollars than you would otherwise. You must resist that temptation and base your decision strictly on the performance of the individual employee.

15

Is There Such a Thing as Motivation?

"I'm gong to get you to do what I want you to do—and like it. But even if you don't like it, you'll do it—and the way I want it done." Basically, that's how a great many managers view the subject of motivation, as a polite word for describing the proper use of authority.

At one time a psychological consulting firm was working in our office. During a feedback session the psychologist assigned to me commented that I was reluctant to use the power of my position to get things done and that I was more interested in persuading people. He meant it as constructive criticism, but I accepted it as a compliment and still do.

I believe one of the greatest strengths of a leader is the ability to get the job done without having to reach back and use the power of the position. I know it's there. I can always reach back and use it if I have to. But isn't the power of the position just as strong if I don't use it? Doesn't my use of the power mean I'm desperate, unable to achieve my objectives in any other way? Clearly, it's more of a resource when I don't use it.

Self-Motivation

The only motivation that really works is self-motivation. When you do a job because you want to, your motivation is self-perpetuating. You don't have to be bludgeoned into doing it. One of the primary responsibilities of a manager is to change the feelings of subordinates from "have to" to "want to."

Also, a good manager gets the job done by finding out how different people respond. If they're self-motivated, they're self-motivated either to get the job done or to just get by. They react in different ways, and you need to understand them well enough to know how they react and to what.

Some people are self-motivated by the possibility of a promotion. As soon as they see a relationship between their current performance and a promotion, they'll strive to perform at the top of their efficiency. Others seek their manager's approval. Since satisfactory performance is how they receive the approval, that's the route they follow. Still others like to compete in a friendly way with their peers. They want to be the best performer in the area and so will work hard at achieving that objective.

Many people are working simply for the dollar, and the way to get more dollars is to perform well to maximize the next salary increase. Many others take great personal pride in doing whatever they do well. Depending on the condition of the labor market, a number of people will be working hard to keep from being unemployed.

Some workers bring their feeling for family into their attitude toward the job, but that's often tied in turn to one of the other reasons I've mentioned—pursuing the dollar. They want to be able to provide more for the family, which requires more dollars.

The Manager's Role

You'll find that learning how to maximize the performance of your people is a permanent, ongoing part of your daily business life. Unless you're in an unusual situation, you'll have turnover, and turnover brings in new people who must be understood. Your obligation in this matter deserves particular emphasis. Your people want to be understood by you. They want to feel important to you as a person—not just as a piece of machinery for getting the work done. Your genuine concern for them will shine through all you do. You don't have to become a parent figure in order to assure them that you understand them and appreciate them. And you don't have to compromise your principles as far as the quality of work is concerned.

Too many managers have the mistaken idea that caring for your people and understanding them indicates a softness or weakness that your subordinates will exploit. They assume (incorrectly) that they will lose control. Just because you care for your people and are interested in their well-being doesn't mean that your people don't have to perform on the job. Concern for and understanding of your staff are signs of management strength, not weakness. The tough, autocratic leader may get satisfactory results for a while, but over the long haul the destroyer will inevitably become the destroyed.

Too many managers believe you can't be fair, concerned, and understanding and still be tough when the situation requires it. You can be. Being fair, concerned, and understanding will make it easier to be tough when the situation demands it. Many managers think that if they're too understanding, they'll be tempted to "cave in" every time a request is made of them. It need not work that way.

In order to establish a proper rapport with your people you have to get to know them. Getting to know them is often a long, ongoing process because of the changes that will occur in personnel and because even the long-term employee's circumstances will change. Because of such changing circumstances, they'll react differently at various phases of their career.

Often, managers will get the idea that they need to be concerned only about new employees. An employee brought up to a satisfactory level of performance, they reason, can be disregarded. This is a mistake. If you don't pay attention to the more seasoned employees, you'll develop problems. The seasoned employee who is doing a satisfactory job will resent being ignored. If you pay attention only to your problem areas, you'll soon find that problems are arising in areas where you didn't expect them.

Employees may reason that the only way to receive any attention from the manager is to be a problem. If seasoned staffers see you using positive, democratic methods to bring the problem employee up to satisfactory standards, they may decide they'd like some of the attention, some of that "stroking." You don't want to allow a situation in which the unsatisfactory performer who is brought up to speed receives more accolades than the satisfactory performer who has been outstanding for years and years. Employees who are never problems need to be told, with regular reinforcement, that their outstanding performance is appreciated and that they are the foundation upon which the department is built.

Don't imagine you can eventually understand everything about the area of self-motivation. There's always more to learn because of the immense variety of personalities you'll meet on the job. One manager I know once told a subordinate that he had a great need for recognition. The manager then refused to give the man that recognition because she considered this need a sign of weakness.

What was wrong, in the first place, was telling the subordinate there was a great need for recognition, as though that were a shortcoming. Such an approach is counterproductive. The manager's objective is to increase the effectiveness of the subordinate and enhance his feeling of contribution and well-being. The manager should have realized that the employee's need for recognition was a readily available management tool. Recognition can be a most effective tool as long as you maintain equity in dealing with your staff.

The Role Played by Titles

This brings me to the subject of titles in an office. Nearly every industry has titles that are peculiar to it and that may not be meaningful to people unfamiliar with the industry. Their significance to people within the industry should not be underestimated.

I've always maintained that titles don't cost a company anything and that you ought to be liberal in using them so long as you can maintain some equity within your organization. By such liberality you not only give recognition to your people but help give them some status within their own community.

The banking industry is well known for this practice, and although some executives in other businesses put them down for it, I think the banks know exactly what they're doing. A customer of a bank dealing with the Vice President—Consumer Loans will feel much more gratified than if dealing with a loan clerk. The spouse of the Vice President—Consumer Loans is surely a greater booster of the bank than the spouse of the loan clerk. In every possible way, the bank's standing in the community is elevated by this liberality with its titles.

The strange thing is that the vice president in this instance may have the same duties as the loan clerk. But which one has the more positive self-image and the stronger self-motivation? The answer is obvious.

As you move up the corporate ladder you may be in a position to influence your company's policy on the use of titles. I sincerely believe you'll get a lot more "house" (recognition) from and for your entire employee group if you use the more liberal approach. Giving someone a title doesn't cost you one thin dime.

Of course, you handle these titles in an orderly fashion. You don't start a new employee off with a super title for a routine position. Rather, the title is out there for the employee to aspire to and achieve in a reasonable length of time.

Show me a company that's parsimonious in its title policy, and I'll show you a company with a management team whose morale can be increased dramatically by a more enlightened use of titles. The impact will be positive even on those who are not yet a part of the management team, because they'll see what they can achieve.

There's nothing wrong with making people feel good about their position and its importance to the organization. Titles can often go a long way toward giving an employee that sense of well-being. I'm amazed at how shortsighted some executives can be on this subject.

An example taken from below the managerial level would be the secretary of a company executive. Instead of using the title of secretary, what's wrong with saying "executive secretary"? Which title is the employee more likely to prefer? Some executives don't want to use *executive secretary* because that would give the employee too inflated a sense of importance. Executives should worry more about making people feel *properly* important than about making them feel *too* important.

Once during a salary freeze, I sensed that the secretary reporting to me was motivated by title and position. I said, "If you have no objection, I'm going to change your title from *secretary* to *staff assistant*." The reaction far exceeded any positive response from previous salary increases.

We all want to feel important, and so do our employees. Let's help them experience that feeling.

The Status Symbol

Another matter that falls in the motivation area is the status symbol. Obviously, status symbols work or they wouldn't find so widespread an application in the business world.

The key to the executive washroom has almost become a joke. I don't understand how anybody can be turned on about this, but perhaps I don't understand the washroom psychology. The size of the office, the luxuriousness of the carpeting, wooden versus steel furniture, executive parking privileges, an executive dining room, company-paid club memberships, company-leased automobiles for executive use, corporate aircraft—the proliferation of status symbols is limited only by the expansiveness of the human imagination.

All could be considered as attempts to inspire people to raise their aspirations. These things are not important in themselves, but indicate that the employee is recognized as having arrived at a certain level in the organization. They're a lot more important to those who don't have them than to those who do. As a friend of mine says about money, "Why is it that most of the people who say money isn't important are just the ones who have plenty of it?" The same goes for status symbols.

A company should not become overly concerned about status symbols, but if it makes them available to its employees, it should not then criticize those same employees for longing after these "methods of keeping score." Actually, for most people, it's not the acquisition of the symbols that's important; it's what they signify to other people. Most status symbols would fall by the wayside if no one else knew you had achieved them.

It's fine to want to attain certain status symbols, but it's important that you keep them in proper perspective. Don't let them become so critical to you that it'll tear you up if you don't attain them as quickly as you think you should.

You cannot substitute status symbols for a satisfactory salary program or a good management approach. Unfortunately, some managers and even some companies think otherwise. They treat people badly or pay them below the competition and then figure they can make up for it with status symbols. Such an attitude is an insult to the intelligence of the subordinate. If the subordinate buys it, the insult is deserved.

Status symbols are the icing on the cake; they are not the cake itself. When used with intelligence and some insight into human behavior, they can be a valuable tool—but a tool is no better than the person using it.

16

The Generation Gap

First-time managers can be, and are, all ages. In my management seminars, I have all sorts of new or prospective managers. Although most are in their twenties or thirties, some have almost as much gray as I have.

In an office environment, we tend to think of managers as being older than the people they supervise. Of course, companies should never base promotions on age, but the fact remains that people who have been around a while have had more experience, have had more time to prove themselves, and are more likely to move into management. Nevertheless, in many offices the managers are younger than the people they supervise—a situation that can be awkward if not handled properly.

Three situations exist with regard to age differences between managers and subordinates: (1) the mature manager supervises people who are younger; (2) the young manager supervises people who are older; and (3) the mature or young manager leads a group of varied ages—some younger, some older, and some of the same generation.

I've found the greatest conflicts occur when a young manager supervises older employees. For some reason, mature people seem to resent working for a young supervisor. Perhaps they feel that the young manager isn't "dry behind the ears."

Most people become managers as a result of promotion within their company. But some older people move into first-time managerial positions because of a career change. It's not as if they had been with a company for thirty years and were now just receiving their first promotion. Often they've had a long career, but one in which they did not manage people. For example, a police officer may retire and then take a second career in which he now will manage the work of others.

This chapter examines the problems that can arise when there is a generation difference between the manager and his subordinates. In particular, I discuss how a young manager can help and inspire his older staff.

Many older workers believe that only experience brings mature judgment. Certainly that is a false premise in many cases. We all know older workers who exercise immature judgment and who constantly make faulty decisions and, conversely, young people who show excellent judgment in almost everything. I have met some young adults who, I suspect, were forty years old when they were born.

A number of years ago, I supervised an employee who had held the same job, with few changes, for thirty years and was proud of the experience this gave her. But actually, she'd had one year's experience thirty times, since her entire job cycle was completed in one year. That's true of many longtime workers.

So if you are managing people older than you, your approach should be nice and easy. You want your staff to think of you as mature beyond your years. If everything you do gives that impression, sooner or later it will become a fact in everyone's mind.

In particular, take your time making changes. Don't immediately throw your weight around and begin to make decisions right and left. That will just create a negative impression that at some point you'll have to counteract. Give older workers time to get used to the idea that you are there, that you are not a threat, and that the world is not going to end. From a management perspective, their lives should be no different from the way they would be if you were twenty years older.

Mistakes to Avoid

In some cases, the young new manager brings a negative initial reaction upon himself by violating the rule of incremental change and using all his newfound authority at once. That practice irritates almost all employees, but it is especially irksome when exhibited by a very young manager. Remember, take it slow and introduce change from the perspective of its potential benefit to all involved.

If direction that might readily be accepted from a mature manager is resented when it comes from a younger one, conclude that the problem must be the messenger, not the message. An older worker who has no confidence in a young manager may not only question the instruction but the reasoning behind it. Of course, this is not fair, but all managers must deal with what people perceive the facts to be.

Too many young managers mistakenly believe that they must immediately answer every question brought to them. They incorrectly believe that any hesitation will be perceived as weakness. Actually, faking it when you don't know *is* a sign of weakness. If you can't answer a question, say "I don't know, but I'll find out." This candor will avoid an image of the know-it-all kid. Remember, in the minds of many older employees, you haven't lived long enough to know it all yet. I'm sure you're familiar with the saying "Those who think they know everything are a real pain to those of us who do."

Many older people may consider a very young manager as someone on the fast track. To get this job at such a tender age, they reason, you must have had some "pull." They may also be convinced that you are only concerned about your own future. To counteract this opinion, demonstrate early on and often that, like all good managers, you are concerned about the well-being of every person reporting to you. As a new manager, you are a salesperson. Your job is to sell your employees on the fact that they are fortunate to have you. You have a mutual interest in helping each other be successful, even though the staff may not feel that way right away.

Many employees like mature managers because they feel they can discuss almost anything with them—something they don't feel about someone young enough to be their son or daughter. As one comic says, "I have underwear older than him." It's unusual for older employees to confide their feelings to a new young manager. There's an inevitable confidence gap, even though sometimes this attitude is not justified.

Strategies for the Young Manager

Make your older employees more comfortable with your supervision by delaying some of the commonsense and fairly obvious decisions you have to make as manager. *You* know that you can make them almost immediately, but when you are new on a job, occasionally postpone your decision when it will do no damage to show your reflection on the matter. For example, if an older employee brings you a problem that he considers serious, but about which you feel you can make an immediate decision, consider saying, "Let me think about that for a while and I'll get back to you tomorrow morning." That way you indicate that you are thoughtful and want to get all the facts, thus dispelling the young, know-it-all image. You also show that you are *not* impetuous, which is another frequent complaint about young managers. That's an interesting "two-fer."

Or, in the same situation, you might consider (with emphasis on the word *consider*) asking, "Do you have a recommendation?" or "What do you think ought to be done?" If the person bringing the problem strikes you as having common sense, give it a try. But if he's someone who builds you a clock when you ask the time, you may be better off passing on this idea.

There is some advantage in reviewing the past performance appraisals of your subordinates when you take on a managerial job, but remember to keep an open mind. The appraisals may be generally correct, but we've all known managers with blind spots about certain staff members. I once inherited an employee who supposedly never had an original idea, but by using a different approach I was able to receive some good ideas from her. So don't give up on people too soon; you may find you have the ability to reach them.

Finally, unless you already know your new, older subordinates personally, consider using last names only until they suggest otherwise. Many mature folks consider younger people too familiar or presumptuous. Of course, if you are being promoted from within an office where everyone uses first names, stick to the norm. However, if you're coming in from outside, try the Mrs. Jones or Mr. Smith approach until you're fully accepted.

17

Helping to Prepare for the Gold Watch

Although helping people prepare for retirement is a company-wide responsibility, your involvement as their supervisor is crucial because to a large extent you represent the company to prospective retirees. You're involved in managing their day-to-day activities and you therefore have the greatest contact with them.

The thought may occur to you that it's a bit odd to be talking about retirement in a book that is aimed at the new manager. It would indeed be odd if we were talking about your own retirement, but since it could happen at any time to someone under your supervision, you must be prepared for it.

I would even suggest that you become acquainted with prospective retirees in your area as soon as you assume your new duties. You'll have to administer the company's program for them. Some companies don't have such a program. In that case your role becomes even more significant.

Many organizations provide graduated time off, over the last few working years, to help the employee get used to the idea of not coming into the office. This may create some work scheduling problems for you as a manager. You can't replace the prospective retiree prematurely, because you want that person to feel needed right up to the day of departure. On the other hand, you can't completely ignore the staffing problems created by the employee's more frequent absences. Some kind of temporary arrangement is best, even if it means using some part-time help. You should not expect your existing staff to pick up the slack unless it can be conveniently handled through duty reassignments.

I know of one situation where a retiring employee—a woman—was told by her male supervisor that she could have virtually unlimited vacation time during her last year on the job. All she had to do was let the supervisor know well in advance when she was going to be gone. This was done. But because he hadn't planned for it, the supervisor had a work-load problem. He reacted by getting miffed at the retiring employee every time she talked about exercising the company policy and taking time off. As a result, she stopped taking the time off. He solved his staffing problem, but he failed as an executive in his responsibility to help this woman prepare for her retirement in the way she had wanted to. That's a rotten solution to a staffing problem. In addition, that employee's recollection of the company is colored by the last year on the job, during which she could not avail herself of what was a stated company policy.

The Company Program

Many companies prepare their employees for retirement through an official company program that's usually administered by the personnel department. In addition to time off, such a program may include individual counseling, discussion of Social Security and Medicare benefits, hobby and craft demonstrations, exploration of the availability of community programs with members of those agencies invited to lead discussions and to answer questions, seminars with trained professionals about the psychology of preparing for retirement, discussions on budget preparation and adjustment to retirement, information about income tax implications for retired people with individual consultation, and any other service that a company may consider appropriate for helping people prepare for this major change in their lifestyle.

If your company does have such a program, you're part of

an enlightened organization and your involvement in the process will be primarily supportive. But if your company has no program, or one that isn't very comprehensive, then your own involvement should become heavier.

However, you shouldn't have much of a problem. Many people who are getting close to retirement look forward to it as the opportunity to do things they haven't had time to do thus far in their lives—and they usually do a good job of preparing themselves for it. Your involvement with them will not be difficult. It will again be primarily a supportive role.

Mandatory and Voluntary Retirement

Except for certain exempt occupations such as airline piloting, law enforcement, and the military, legislation now prohibits mandatory retirement. An individual can work as long as he wants, and stays productive.

The employee who doesn't want to retire and who dreads that terrible day is tough to work with. Such people, if they are no longer productive, often see themselves as being rewarded for thirty years of faithful service by being "put out to pasture." Work is their life. You can help such people by listening to them and making suggestions as to where they might find part-time work after retirement. The most valuable service you can provide is your sympathetic attention so that they can talk about their feelings as they try to adjust to the inevitable.

Before mandatory retirement at a given age was forbidden by law, there was much controversy about the concept. Frankly, there were valid arguments on both sides of the question. The fact that the law was changed does not destroy the validity of the issues, and people working in management still have to deal with them.

If everyone were required to retire at a specified age, everyone would be treated the same. Knowing when someone was going to retire would give younger people in the organization some knowledge about when certain promotional opportunities would occur. That way, training and development could be planned on an orderly basis. In addition, judgments about the continued competency of those who work to more advanced ages would not have to be made.

Another advantage of everyone's retiring at the same age is that "the system" determines when people retire; it isn't management deciding when someone has to hang it up because they are no longer as productive as the job requires. This situation gets sticky when the employee believes that the quality and the quantity of her performance are still satisfactory, but when management and the facts indicate otherwise.

One strong argument against any mandatory retirement age is that individuals with valuable experience are lost to the company. Many older workers are alert, in satisfactory health, and able to work for additional years. Retirement, the argument goes, should be based on competency. People who are able to get the job done should be allowed to work as long as they can produce.

However, the removal of a mandatory retirement age creates the potential for bitter feelings and resentment. Employees who want to continue working, but are told to retire because of deteriorating performance, feel as though they are being fired. That is not the way to end a long and distinguished career. Nevertheless, the employee who continues to work indefinitely must recognize the potential for this kind of ending. I'm reminded of outstanding entertainers who cannot give up when they are at their peak. As their powers diminish, they become pathetic figures, still looking for adulation and applause. The few who remain at the top are rare. How much better to go while the audience is still clamoring for just one more.

Your Own Role

As the employee gets closer to retirement, you should indicate that you're available for consultations about the event. You show your interest by calling the employee into your office and asking how his retirement plans are coming along. Some executives tell employees, "You know my door is always open. If you're having any problems, be sure to come in." Most employees will not respond to that kind of invitation. Rather, they'll view it as a polite brushoff. Unless they have a serious problem to talk over with you, there's a good chance they won't come in.

You must take the initiative. Don't wait for prospective retirees to come in on their own. Most of them will not want to bother you with what they might consider chit-chat. They may think you're too busy for them even though you are not. You're never too busy for your people.

Periodically, call such an employee into your office. If you have the facilities, share a cup of coffee. You can start off with such a simple question as "How is your planning for retirement coming along?" If that doesn't get the conversation going, keep probing until you find a subject that does generate some interest. If you know the employee well, you will know the keys to initiating a friendly conversation. If you don't, a few discreet inquiries in the department will provide some answers.

Here are several other questions that may get the employee to open up and start talking.

"How does your husband [wife] feel about your retirement?"

"Do you have any trips planned for your retirement?"

"Have you worked out your retirement budget as yet?"

"Do you plan on continuing to live in this area after you retire?"

"How do your children feel about your retirement? Do they have a positive attitude about it?"

"What one aspect of retirement do you think about the most?"

I'm sure you can think of many other questions that will help to initiate conversation.

The fact is that what may start out as a low-key, casual conversation may turn into a more serious discussion about the real concerns the prospective retiree has on his or her mind.

Many managers feel that the "out of sight, out of mind" approach is better. They incorrectly reason that they are asking for problems and that enough problems exist without seeking them out. The question is then whether they find out about the problems or not. Your interest in listening to your subordinates' plans for the future and learning about their misgivings as they move into the retirement phase of their life could be very helpful to them. Don't deny them that benefit.

Four
Preparing and Improving Yourself

18

"How Am I Doing?"

My comments to this point should have convinced you that I believe you have a fairly high opinion of your own capacities and that it's not an unduly inflated viewpoint.

It seems to me that people get awfully mixed up in dealing with this ego thing. There are always those around who want you to feel guilty if you have a high opinion of yourself. Rather, I say, "Love your neighbor as yourself." This implies that your capacity to love your neighbor is determined by your capacity to love yourself. I think the principle applies in management too.

Your Self-Image

Many excellent books have been written on the subject of self-image, and they have important concepts in them for the manager. Perhaps I can share a few basics that I believe will help you in your managerial career.

The fact is, we fall or rise by our self-image. If we have a low opinion of ourselves and believe we're going to fail, our subconscious will try to deliver that result to us. Conversely, if we have a high opinion of ourselves and think we're going to succeed, our chances for success are greatly increased. I realize that's an oversimplification, but it conveys the thought. If you think success, if you look successful, if you're confident of being successful, you greatly increase your chances to be successful. It's primarily a matter of attitude. If you believe you're a failure, that's what you're likely to be.

To reinforce a successful attitude you need some success along the way. Now that you've moved into your first managerial position, every success you have will serve as a building block to further achievements.

It should be obvious that you can't substitute feelings of success for actual accomplishments. You can't have the appearance without any substance. That would be a sham. You'll soon be found out, and to your own disadvantage.

An Impression of Arrogance

One of the most serious problems that I've observed in newly appointed young managers is the impression they give of arrogance. Be careful that you don't handle your feeling of success so that it's misconstrued as arrogance. A manager can feel pride in having been elevated into the managerial ranks without appearing cocky and arrogant. Rather, the impression conveyed should be one of *quiet confidence.*

Do you suspect that there are people in your organization who don't believe you were the right selection and who'd delight in your failure? That's not only possible, it's quite likely. An appearance that can be construed as arrogance is going to convince these people that they're correct in their assessment of you.

Handling Mistakes

In carrying out your duties as a manager, you'll occasionally make mistakes. You'll exercise bad judgment. This happens to all of us. How you view these mistakes is important in your own development. Be completely honest with yourself and everyone you associate with. Don't try to cover up a mistake, rationalize it, or, what is even worse, blame it on a subordinate. New executives have difficulty accepting responsibility for the mistakes of subordinates. Here again we meet the "octopus" managers discussed in Chapter 1. So skittish are such managers about mistakes that they decide to avoid criticism by handling all the more complex work themselves. When you do this, you shut off your promotion possibilities and you may even kill yourself with overwork. A frightening prospect!

So it's difficult for many young leaders to learn to accept responsibility for the mistakes of subordinates. It's a matter of self-image. The way to solve the problem is to build your entire managerial role. You solve it by being a better trainer, by being a better selector of people, by developing better internal controls that minimize the mistakes and their impact. The way you view your department and your staff will have a great influence on how you view yourself.

Self-Infatuation and Self-Contradiction

You have to put forth your best image, but don't be so successful at it that, like the movie star, you fall for your own publicity. Be willing to admit to yourself what your shortcomings are. You'd be surprised at how many executives can't do that. They of course have shortcomings. They can't be experts at everything. But in ascending to their exalted position, they find that everyone starts catering to them. It takes an unusual executive to realize that all that honorific treatment doesn't increase intelligence or boost knowledge. It's easy and pleasant to sit back and accept all that bowing and scraping. The executive is soon convinced that the adoration is deserved. Perhaps the charisma you think is personal is created by the position you hold.

The *infallibility syndrome* becomes most noticeable at the level of chief executive officer. Between the beginning manager and the top post are varying degrees of infallibility that seem to go with the job. You have to keep an honest perspective on who you are. If tomorrow you were named CEO, you wouldn't automatically become smarter than you were yesterday. But people would start listening to you as though you were one of the Three Wise Men. You didn't get smarter; you just gained more power. Don't confuse the two!

Pay little attention to what executives say in this regard. Pay more attention to what they do. If an executive says, "I hire people who are smarter than me," think about what the words mean. If the executive says, "I encourage my people to disagree with me; I don't want to be surrounded by yes-men," remember what happened last week when the executive snapped off the head of a subordinate who disagreed. The words are contradicted by the actions.

Throughout your business life you'll encounter executives who espouse beautiful management philosophies. The only problem is that they wield their authority using other philosophies. So be honest with yourself; recognize what you are and try to get your "management talk" reasonably close to your "management performance."

Shortcomings and Prejudices

I don't mean you should advertise your weaknesses. But be willing to admit them to yourself, and do all you can to shore them up. For example, I've always found that the things I don't do well are also the things I don't much like doing. Now that can hardly be a coincidence. But you'll get through those chores you don't like if you do them early when your energy levels are at their height. Every job has aspects to it that you're not going to like; get them done and out of the way so you can do the parts of the job that are the most challenging, the most creative, and the most fun.

Some people like the routine and repetitive parts of the job best. If that's the way you are, then I question whether you should be moving into management and aspiring to even greater responsibilities. It's rarely a problem, because people who like routine tasks seldom move into management. When they do, it's usually a minidisaster.

In addition to recognizing your shortcomings as they apply to your job, be willing to admit attitudes of yours that may be a problem. For example, I'm prejudiced against second-generation wealth. I'm perfectly convinced that people with inherited wealth would fail if they had to start from the bottom like the rest of us. I have to work really hard at overcoming my prejudice when I deal with these people and am forced to view them as equals. My prejudice tells me they're not equals—they're inferior. Conversely, I'm biased in favor of people like myself, who came from a poverty background and worked their way up.

Objectivity

Another aspect of your self-image is the ability to be objective. Through the years I've known a great many managers who tell you they're looking at the problem objectively and then proceed to explain their attitudes or solutions in an almost entirely subjective way. When a manager starts off by claiming to be completely objective, ask yourself why the statement was made. Usually, it's an attempt not only at deception but at self-deception. Executives make subjective decisions and then "cover their trail" by telling everyone how objective they were about them. I don't know of anyone who can be completely objective. I have found, however, that the higher the position, the greater the likelihood that subjectivity will be called objectivity.

I bring up this matter because it will help you to analyze how you yourself should view the problem as a manager. "What attitudes, prejudices, or experiences do I have that might cause me to be unnecessarily subjective? How can I approach this problem to discount these subjective considerations, granting that I can't completely purge myself of them? Is my decision fair? Can I defend the decision if I have to?" If you're satisfied with your answers to those questions, then don't agonize over your decisions. And once they're made, don't second-guess yourself, because the vast majority of the decisions will be correct.

Quiet Confidence

Develop quiet confidence about your decision-making ability. As you make more and more decisions, you get better at it. Decisions don't require Solomon-like wisdom; they require the ability to develop the facts. The critical point is to know when you have enough information to make the decision. Generally speaking, if you can get 70 to 80 percent of the information you need, you can make the decision. The inordinate amount of time you'd spend getting the rest of the information would in all probability not result in a different decision anyway. The delay in making the decision is usually more costly than the risk of making a decision on the basis of insufficient information.

The impulsive decision maker leans the other way and makes decisions before an adequate amount of information is obtained. Young managers sometimes believe they have to be fast decision makers to be successful. It will take experience to get a feel for when you have adequate information to make the decision.

View yourself as a person who isn't afraid to make decisions, but who's also constantly learning the process. This is an area where you need to strike a balance. You don't want to shoot from the hip in making decisions, but you don't want to go to the opposite extreme and never get your gun out of the holster either. Finding that balance will be a learning process. Eventually you'll get to the point where you'll instinctively know when the decision can and should be made.

In summary, view yourself as honestly as you can. Don't be the kind of person who finds reasons for decisions after they've been made. Don't make emotional judgments and rationalize them afterward. When you do that, you'll find yourself defending decisions you wish you hadn't made. All of us delude ourselves to some extent, but we help ourselves by holding it down to a bare minimum.

Promotion and Self-Promotion

As mentioned in an earlier chapter, you're judged by the performance of your division, department, or other applicable organizational unit; the people who report to you are therefore more important to your future than the people you report to. That leads directly to the matter of office politics, which comes into play more in the process of scratching your way up the organization ladder than in any other situation.

Office Politics: Playing the Game

Some people are viewed as "cold turkeys" by those who report to them but as "warm, generous human beings" by their superiors. Such people are really playing the game, but in the long run they're sure to fail. However much they may succeed in fulfilling their ambitions at the office, they'll fail as human beings.

If getting promoted is more important to you than your integrity, than being your own person, then I would recommend that you skip the rest of this chapter because you won't like much of what is said in it.

I maintain that almost anyone can succeed temporarily by being an opportunist, but consider the price that's been paid in getting there. Granted that many of the decisions made about promotions will not seem fair to you, and that they won't all be made on the basis of ability. No one guaranteed you that life would be fair, so don't expect it.

I'm not saying that most promotions are made on the basis of something other than fairness and ability. But even though most companies do try to make these decisions fairly, it doesn't always come off that way. Besides, a decision that seems perfectly rational to the executive making it may not seem rational to you, especially if you thought you were the likely candidate for the promotion.

In spite of that, to get promoted you still have to prepare yourself for it. If you depend on luck or serendipity, your chances are greatly diminished. You have everything to gain and nothing to lose by being prepared. Who knows, your opportunity for promotion may come from outside your company. You want to be prepared for that possibility too.

Preparing Your Understudy

As soon as you've mastered your job, you must start looking for an understudy. The reason for this is clear. If the company refuses to consider candidates to replace you, it may view you as indispensable in your current position and you may be passed up for promotion.

Finding the appropriate understudy can be a delicate matter. You should not select your crown prince or princess too early. If the candidate doesn't develop properly and fails to demostrate the skills needed to move into your job, you could have a serious problem at hand. Changing your mind about a successor you've already selected is like opening a can of worms.

How you go about preparing for your own replacement is of critical importance. If you already have an assistant who's perfectly capable in the job, then it's a matter of helping that assistant develop as thoroughly and as rapidly as possible.

Give your assistant bits and pieces of your job to perform. Under no circumstance should you delegate your entire job to your assistant and then sit back and read newspapers and business magazines. The company obviously didn't put you in the position for that purpose.

Allow your assistant to do more and more aspects of your job until most of it has been learned. Make sure the assistant does each section of the job frequently enough that it won't be forgotten. Occasionally, invite the assistant to participate in the interviewing process when you're hiring new employees.

Assuming the assistant is performing satisfactorily, start your political campaign for your prospective replacement. Make sure your boss knows how well the man or woman is developing. On performance appraisals, use such terms as "promotable" and "is developing into an outstanding management prospect." Of course, never say these things if they're untrue; that would probably work to the disadvantage of both you and your assistant. But if the assistant is developing well, communicate it up to the next level without being blatant about it.

You run the risk that the assistant might get promoted out from under you. It's of course a risk worth taking. Even if this happens to you several times, you'll get the reputation of being an outstanding developer of people. That will add to your own promotability. Besides, you'll find that developing subordinates can be a very highly satisfying experience. And while you're worrying about preparing your people for promotion, it's hoped that your own boss is just as concerned about you and your future.

Multiple Choice

If you don't have an assistant already in place, you should assign parts of your job to several people and see how they run with the added responsibility and the new opportunity. This is indeed to your advantage, since training several replacements at once makes it unlikely that all the candidates will get promoted out from under you. This in-depth backstopping will serve you well in emergencies.

Don't be in too big a hurry to move a single candidate into the position of assistant. The moment you name a person as your assistant, others stop striving for the job. That's the trouble with any promotion. Those who don't get it stop aspiring to it, and that usually has an adverse effect on their performance, even though it may be temporary.

Here's a management concept that may be of value to you: Always hold something out for your subordinates to aspire to. If you get to the point where you have to select a single subordinate as your heir apparent, then let the losing candidates know that opportunities still exist for them in other departments, and that you'll help them toward their goal of a promotion.

But as long as you continue to have several prospects vying for the position, you must treat them as equals. Rotate the assignments among them. Make sure that all of them get exposed to all aspects of your job. If you're gone from the office occasionally, put each in charge of the operation in turn. Give them all a chance at managing the personnel aspects of the job too.

On some regular basis, meet with all the candidates at once and discuss your job with them. Don't say, "Let's discuss my job"; rather, talk about some specific problems they've encountered. All of them will benefit from the discussion. If one of them had to face an unusual management problem in your absence, why shouldn't all of them profit from the experience?

The Perils of Indispensability

Again let me point out the importance of not allowing yourself to become indispensable. Some executives trap themselves into this kind of situation. In their effort to ensure the quality of the work, they request that all difficult questions be referred to them. It doesn't take long for employees to figure out that anything out of the ordinary will soon be going to you as the boss. It isn't the time taken from your day that creates problems. The more fundamental trouble is that your people soon stop trying to work out the more complex problems by themselves.

I believe it's important that your people be encouraged to find answers on their own. They'll be better employees for it. There are limits, of course, to the areas of responsibility that can be delegated to them, but I've always felt that you're better off erring on the side of too much latitude in delegating responsibility than too little. I think it's good management to allow staff members some responsibility while still assuring them that the executive is accountable for their performance.

I'm sure you've heard people worrying about whether the company would get along without them while they're on vacation. They have it backward: Their real worry is that the company *will* get along just fine without them. The executive who's doing the right kind of job in developing employees and backup management can leave with the assurance that the department will function very smoothly in his or her absence. The truly efficient and dedicated executive, indeed, has progressed to the point where he or she can even be gone permanently—to a promotion in another company. I've known managers who, in a misguided view of what their job required, made themselves indispensable and spent the rest of their business careers proving it—by never being moved from that position.

The main problem with such people is that they don't understand what the job of management is about. Management isn't doing—it's seeing that it's done.

The Lazy Employee

Another practice I'd like to recommend is that of indulging the lazy employee. Before you think I've completely lost my mind, let me explain. The lazy employees I've known are ceaselessly on the lookout for easier ways to do things. People who enjoy detail and busywork are not going to find out ways to eliminate them—because that's their thing. Not so with the lazy employee, who'll work hard and long at finding an easier way to do the job.

If you provide me with industrious people who like fussing endlessly over minute trivia, I'll never be able to reduce staff. However, sprinkle my staff with a few lazy souls and eventually I'll be able to reduce the number of employees. As some people leave, I won't have to replace them. And I know well that the line going straight to upper management's heart is "reduce staff and cost."

Your Predecessor

It helps a great deal if your predecessor in the job was a real dunderhead who left the place in a shambles. Unless you're a complete idiot, you'll look like a champion by comparison. That's preferable to stepping into a smooth-running operation. What you can do with statistics alone is amazing. So if you ever have a choice between moving into an area that appears to be in chaos and moving into a nice clean operation, go into the chaos each and every time. You'll never regret it.

Continuing Your Education

Something else you should consider in preparing yourself for promotion is to extend your knowledge about the business you're in. It's not enough to beome expert in your restricted area of responsibility. You must understand more about your company's entire operation.

You can acquire this additional knowledge in several ways. For instance, you can broaden your knowledge through selected readings. Your own boss may be able to recommend published material that fits closely into your own company's operation and philosophy. No boss is ever insulted when asked for advice. However, a word of caution: Don't ask for advice too often, because your boss will either suspect you can't make up your own mind about too many things or figure you're seeking a favor. Neither of these reactions will help your cause.

If your company offers education programs, sign up for them. Even if you can't see any immediate benefit from them, they'll serve you well over the long haul. In addition, you're displaying an eagerness to learn.

Dress

A few thoughts about proper dress might be appropriate. Styles come and go, so what is appropriate at one time may seem highly inappropriate a few years (or even a few months) later. Obviously, what you wear as a manager in a factory is altogether different from what you wear in an office. My point is, if you are going to be successful, it helps to look successful.

When I run to the store in the sloppy work clothes I've been wearing to clean the garage, I'm treated with much less courtesy and respect than when I'm dressed in a suit, shirt, tie, and dress shoes. The gray at the temples doesn't seem to do anything for me when I'm in jeans. That may not be the way it ought to be, but that's my experience. A rule of thumb is this: If you're not sure of what to wear, you're better off erring on the side of overdressing than underdressing.

Tooting Your Own Horn—But Softly

A point about playing personal politics is in order here. You can be the greatest thing since graham crackers, but if you're the only one who knows it, you won't go anywhere with your many talents. So not only should you make sure your achievements are known to the persons you report to, you should go about spreading the glad tidings in the most effective way possible. However, if you're obviously tooting your own horn, people are going to react negatively. You must be subtle. Keep in mind that no one's interest in your promotability coincides with your own.

For example, let's say the local community college is offering courses that you think would help you perform your job and become more promotable. You might sign up for one of these courses and complete it satisfactorily, yet no one in your organization would ever know about it. Let's assume the course you're taking is in accounting. Here are some ways to make sure your boss and the company know you're taking the course:

- Send a note to the personnel department—and a carbon copy to your boss—asking that your personnel records show you're taking the course. This puts the information in your personnel file, where anyone examining your record and considering you for promotion will see it. On completing the course, again notify the personnel department of the achievement.

- Use the casual conversation approach with your boss: "One of the fellas in my accounting class said something funny last night. . . ." The boss will ask, "What accounting class?"

- Place books on your desk that will prompt the desired question.

- Ask your boss for clarification of a class discussion item that you didn't fully understand.

- Invite a classmate to the office to have lunch with you and introduce her to your boss: "Mr. Smith, I'd like you to meet my accounting course classmate, Nelda Jones."

I'm sure you get the idea. The more subtle you become in your self-advertisement, the less likely that it will appear as horn tooting.

With an apology to the King James version of the Bible, "What profit it a man if he becometh the most qualified employee in the company and no one else knoweth it?" You must develop communications techniques because too few bosses will approach you and say, "Tell me, what are you doing to prepare yourself for promotion?"

Some people may react negatively when I talk about being political. The word connotes making backroom deals and compromising principles in order to get ahead. That kind of politics does, of course, exist in an office too. Some of it can be funny and some of it can be very vicious. But in speaking of preparing yourself for promotion, I'm using the word *political* in its finest sense. I mean making sure your superior characteristics and accomplishments are known to those who make the promotion decisions. This is being political in a positive way; you could just as easily refer to it as commonsense communication.

Some executives blithely announce that if you do your job to the best of your ability, the promotions and raises will take care of themselves. But if your superiors don't know what you're doing, how can they take your accomplishments into consideration in making their promotion decision? You'll often hear executives mouthing clichés that they think are great pearls of wisdom. At least two things may be wrong about some of the clichés: The executive saying them doesn't manage that way, and the statements are no longer true. The bit about the raises and the promotions taking care of themselves applies here.

You must develop your own style of communicating the important aspects of your development in the company, but you must see to it that the way you get the message across doesn't offend others or make you appear pushy.

But Is the Game Worth the Candle?

Working toward a promotion is a constant in every executive's career—unless, of course, you're the kind of person who reaches a certain point and then loses interest in moving further. There's surely nothing wrong with the attitude "I don't want to pay the price of moving to the next rung of the ladder." That's indeed healthier than finding out too late that your assumption that you're still promotable is not shared by management.

Unfortunately, in too many cases, you're never told, so you keep on busting your butt to be promoted and don't know that your chances are nil. One reason, I suspect, is that your superiors know how valuable you are in the present job and they don't want to lose you, even though they feel you've topped out. Sometimes the awful reality doesn't dawn on you until you're almost at the age when another promotion is unlikely.

You have a right to know where you stand in the company, and I see absolutely nothing wrong with pressing for the information before it's too late. If you think top management is wrong in judging you nonpromotable, there are things you can do about it. One way is to seek additional challenge by changing jobs; another is to supplement your job with new, additional challenges—hobbies and social or civic activities— that will make your life more interesting and rewarding.

A word of caution: Don't spend a lot of time worrying about promotion until you have a solid handle on your current job. Mastery of that job is your first priority. Only then should you start your campaign to get promoted. It really is a campaign, although primarily a one-person effort. Others with nearly as much interest in your getting promoted are subordinates who believe they have a shot at your position once you've moved up.

Don't start making noises about promotability too soon. Your boss may consider it premature. You've finally got things in your area going smoothly; the boss can now relax a bit—the company's investment in you is paying off. However, if all of a sudden you start talking about moving on to something better, the boss will consider you an impatient ingrate. Promotion, of course, often crosses your mind, but some things are best kept to yourself for a while.

You may have a master plan. You may have a particular ultimate goal in mind. It may even be the chief executive officer's position. But you must proceed by aiming your sights on interim goals. You must perform each of the assignments in super fashion if you're to move on to your next goal. Each of the steps along the way to your final goal becomes critically important. Each offers a reassessment opportunity. At each step you must determine whether you're willing to pay the price required to get you to the next step. There's nothing wrong with deciding the price is too high and that you don't want to pay it.

I've observed, however, that not every step up the ladder requires that you pay a higher price. Sometimes that's just propaganda put out by people in higher positions to prove to everyone else that they deserve to be there. So in making your way to the next position up the ladder toward your goal, be prepared for dense diversionary smoke screens. And assuming it does require paying an additional price, weigh that price against the reward the higher position promises. Is the game worth the candle?

The Job You Want

In analyzing the position you aspire to accurately, you may find that the person holding it is a workaholic. Many of the tasks workaholics perform are occupational hobbies, indulged in compulsively—every weekend and every night. Sometimes these people are escaping from pressures at home, even though they'd be the last to admit it. Working at the office is a socially acceptable way of staying away from home. Sometimes your workaholic boss is poor at delegating authority and thus cannot significantly decrease the burdens of the position. But just because a situation exists doesn't mean it has to be that way.

Obviously it's not up to you to tell your supervisor that she appears to be working harder than the job actually requires. At this point let's admit that to some extent all of us attempt to make ourselves look a bit more important or our jobs look a bit tougher than they really are. We all want to be cast in as favorable a light as possible.

Seeking Advice

The one person who can realistically view the job you aspire to is the predecessor of the incumbent. That person has the distance and disinterest to give you candid answers to your questions. That person also will outrank you by at least two levels on the organization chart and in all likelihood will be older than you. How you approach this executive will largely determine the kind of response you'll get. Again, don't make the approach too quickly if you're still fairly new in your current position.

However, let's assume that a respectable length of time has passed and you've decided you're going to approach Mr. Hunter. You don't approach him at all if he stands directly in the chain of command as it affects you personally. That is, if Mrs. Rogers holds the job you aspire to, and if she reports directly to Mr. Hunter and you report directly to her, under no circumstances do you go around her to talk to Mr. Hunter about the job she holds. I'm assuming here that Mrs. Rogers does not report to Mr. Hunter. It's even better if Mrs. Rogers is not your boss. You have to sort out these lines of reporting in your own company and make the decision on whether or not to talk to Mr. Hunter. I'm assuming you exercise sound judgment in these matters. In any case, the decision is made: You're going to talk to Mr. Hunter. How do you approach him and what do you say to set the stage properly?

As mentioned earlier, most managers or executives are flattered when asked for advice. Your opening might go something like this:

"Mr. Hunter, I'd like to get the benefit of your experience. In looking around at positions in the company that I think I'd like to aspire to, I've found that the job Mrs. Rogers holds might be a challenging one. I know you held that position at one time. Did you find it a challenging and interesting aspect of your career? Do you think it's reasonable for me to aspire to that job?"

You may not be able to get it all out as a nonstop monologue, but at least you've put the matter on the agenda. You then sit back, remain silent, and let Mr. Hunter lay his wisdom on you.

Let's analyze the recommended opening gambit. First of all, you've asked your superior for the benefit of his experience. You've thereby put him in a generous frame of mind. Second, you've stated that you've been looking around at positions in the company that you might aspire to. This indicates that your horizons are broad; you haven't limited your search to the area you're currently working in. Third, you didn't say to Mr. Hunter that the job Mrs. Rogers holds *is* a challenging position; you said it *might be* a challenging one. You're going to let Mr. Hunter tell *you* about the challenge in the job. After all, you want the benefit of his experience.

You then asked him if he found the job interesting. If he had found it to be a dull, methodical job that bored the hell out of him, that's information you ought to have. From there you went on to ask him if he thought it was reasonable for you to aspire to the job. How he answers that question will depend on how well he knows you and the kind of performer you are in your current position.

You might also go directly to Mrs. Rogers. As in the preceding example, this depends on several factors, including where you and Mrs. Rogers are relative to each other on the organization chart. Here again your judgment will have to prevail. But sometimes the direct approach is bold enough to be quite effective:

"Mrs. Rogers, I wonder if I could ask your advice on a matter of my own personal development. I know the company always has its eye out for people who are promotable, and I'm positive that if there's a list of promotable people you're on it. I'm interested in having a shot at your job when you're promoted. I'd like to find out your feelings about your job and also whether you think it's reasonable for me to aspire to it."

Again, you may not be able to deliver the monologue eloquently, without stumbling, but it's the kind of language you want to start with.

In this opener with Mrs. Rogers, you first asked for advice. You can expect a favorable response. Second, you told her you think she's going somewhere in the organization. She certainly won't find that offensive. Third, you didn't say you wanted her job when she was promoted. You merely said you wanted a shot at it—a fair chance. Who could object to that? You then asked if she thought it was reasonable for you to aspire to the job. As one of my attorney friends says, you knew the answer before you asked the question.

Both the conversation with Mr. Hunter and the one with Mrs. Rogers require finesse and self-assurance.

Acquiring a Sponsor

One favorable side effect of such a conversation is the acquisition of a *sponsor*. It can't hurt to have executive power on your side. In fact, being sponsored by a couple of people higher in the organization who are stars themselves is a great thing to have going for you.

Most sponsors are acquired by careful cultivation. Few sponsors get the idea on their own. Something had to happen to give them the thought; usually it was a favorable impression you created one way or another.

Style and Merit

Achieving the objectives discussed in this chapter requires satisfactory performance on your part and confidence in yourself. Often, the difference between a satisfactory job and a great job is image or style. I believe your style colors a superior's perception of your performance, especially if the style is one your superior reacts positively to. But a bad or offensive style is similarly critical in evoking a negative response.

There's a vast difference between doing a great job and maximizing the mileage you get out of that, on the one hand, and conning people into thinking you're doing an outstanding job when you're not cutting the mustard, on the other. I'm assuming you're capable; you're making your way up the organization ladder on your merits.

19

Organizing Your Own Time

Have you ever gone home from the office with the feeling that you didn't accomplish any of the things you wanted to get done that day? We all have days like that, spent entirely in putting out brushfires. Sometimes it can't be helped, but if it's happening to you regularly, part of the problem may be your own lack of organization.

My Own Approach

My own approach toward this book is a good example. Almost every day I'd set a goal of writing a full chapter, yet an entire week would sometimes go by without my having written a single line. The reason was the compulsion I felt to block out several solid hours so I could tackle a chapter. The sytem got me nowhere. Then I decided that my effort had to be broken up into smaller pieces. So my goal became to write two hand-written pages each day. Occasionally I'd miss a day; I then set a goal of four pages for the next day.

As a result of the change in emphasis, I started getting material written, even though the demands on my time from other responsibilities had not changed. The only change was my attitude toward and approach to the problem. One evening I sat down to write my two pages—and ended up writing a dozen. If I had established a goal for that day of twelve pages, I wouldn't even have begun to write that evening because of the lateness of the hour.

The List

A number of years ago I read an article about the late American industrialist Henry Kaiser. Among his many achievements was the establishment of a company that built cargo vessels called Liberty ships during World War II. These ships were completely constructed in a matter of days, truly a spectacular accomplishment.

The first thing Kaiser did on entering the office in the morning was to sit at his desk with a legal-size pad on which he listed the items he wished to accomplish that day. I don't recall that he attempted to list them in a priority order. During the day, the list remained on top of the desk. As a goal was accomplished, a line was drawn through it on the pad. Goals that didn't get accomplished that day would be put on the next day's list.

I tried this simple approach to organizing my day and was pleasantly surprised at how much more I started to accomplish. You're forced to plan the day's activities as you write the day's objectives on the pad. That's probably the greatest value of the technique.

There are several different approaches that can be used in planning your day. Some managers believe they ought to list the objectives in the order of their importance and complete them in that sequence. Others prefer making three lists. The first contains emergency matters that are bleeding for attention. The second comprises items that are not emergency in nature but have to be done. The third includes things that can be done when you have the time. This is a fine arrangement if your day is so highly controlled that you need not worry about being deterred from making your appointed rounds by unexpected circumstances.

Such a regimented day has never been possible for me. I can't control the interruptions. I can't shut off the telephone. So I just make my little daily list of every variety of objectives, from dealing with emergencies to planning long-range projects that I'm hoping to get around to someday. Included are matters that are putting no pressure on me at the moment.

Another reason for not breaking my list down into categories is my knowledge of what has to be done immediately and what can wait. Let's face it, I know I can't survive as a manager if I ignore my emergencies. So even if the emergency is number twenty on my list, I'm not going to take care of nineteen other tasks ahead of the panic item.

Anyone else looking at my list would probably think I had lost my mind, because I write objectives down as they enter my head without worrying about any order or priority for accomplishing them. I'll even put personal items on the list, like reminding myself that I'm supposed to stop at the grocery store for a loaf of bread on my way home. A long-range project may appear on my list every day for a couple of months. Eventually, I'll get tired of repeatedly listing it and I'll get it done. I start feeling like a procrastinator if I keep it on my list too long.

I also get a psychological lift out of drawing a line through tasks that have been completed. It's great to sit there late in the afternoon reflecting on the day's activities and see that the majority of the items on your list have been accomplished.

Don't throw the list away when you leave the office. The next morning, yesterday's list will serve two purposes. It will remind you of all you accomplished the day before—there's nothing wrong with that—and will inform you of what remained unaccomplished. These latter items then go on the new list. That's especially important for long-range projects that might get accidentally dropped from the list. Too many creative ideas and projects get away from us because we didn't write them down.

I remember reading once that the late Duke Ellington kept paper and pencil on his night table for use in jotting down musical ideas that would come to him in bed at night. I'm sure you've had the experience I've often had: A great thought comes to you in the middle of the night, but in the morning you find that it's gone. No matter how you strain to recapture it, it eludes you and you can't bring it back.

Homework

Nowadays, nearly every executive (junior and senior) carries an attaché case to and from the office. I'll admit right here that I carry an attaché case back and forth between my home and the office, even though I seldom take any work home with me.

In a smaller city it may be convenient to go back into the office at night. In metropolitan areas this is usually not an option, so the executive either stays late or takes work home. You should not be taking routine work home on a regular basis. If you are, it may well be that you're poorly organized. Taking creative work home makes sense since the more quiet environment (if it is more quiet) does lend itself to creative pursuits.

My attaché case contains things I want with me whether I'm at home or at the office. I'm developing a list to the port side from carrying it all these years.

My Day at the Office

In preparing your daily list, you have to decide what will be done in what order. As mentioned earlier, you'll almost certainly take care of the emergencies first. You'll then glance over the list and decide what to do next. My own usual procedure is to do things I don't like and get them out of the way, thus freeing myself to do what I enjoy. I often move very early to a task I can complete quickly, thereby setting myself up mentally in an accomplishing spirit. Even though I know full well that I'm psyching myself, it still works.

Every once in a while all hell will immediately break loose when I arrive at the office, and I won't get to make my list. Riding home in my car, I may have the uncomfortable feeling that I didn't accomplish a great deal that day. That kind of thing happened more frequently earlier in my career. Making my list has now become a habit, and it's a rare day indeed when my list doesn't get made.

The Weekend List

My wife was a list maker long before I had read about Henry Kaiser's approach—she makes lists of things she wants me to do around the house on weekends. Fortunately, she did not make a list every weekend. However, I've become so habitual a list maker that I now make the weekend list of house chores myself. I don't necessarily transfer uncompleted chores to next weekend's list—there's no sense in carrying this passion for order and efficiency too far.

The Closed Period

Some organizations follow a "closed-office" procedure you may want to use in mapping out your own day to accomplish more. For example, an office will have a two-hour-closed period, where it's business as usual except that no one in the office goes to see anyone else. No one makes interoffice phone calls and no company meetings are ever scheduled during this closed period. Genuine emergencies are handled expeditiously; calls from clients, customers, or other outsiders are accepted.

The idea has a great deal of merit. It means you'll have two hours each day when no one from within the company is going to call you on the phone or come into your office. It gives you an opportunity to control what you do during the specified period. Perhaps some person got the idea while working in the office on a weekend and noticing how much more was accomplished then than in the same period of time during the week. But the idea is feasible only if you don't shut off your customers or clients during the closed period. It's an idea an entire organization can use to advantage.

Remembering and Reflecting

Here's a bit of advice that won't do a whole lot for you at the office but will help you remember things you're supposed to stop for on the way home. Put a reminder in the pocket where you keep your car keys. Then, on your way to the parking lot at the end of the workday, you'll reach into your pocket for the car keys and presto!—there it is. Maybe you don't get distracted from doing personal errands the way I do; you may therefore not need to have such reminders. I do.

A final suggestion about how best to organize your time: Plan to have a quiet period each day. You may not get it every day, but it's important that you set aside some time for daydreaming and reflection. It's vital to the inner person. Also, problems that seem insurmountable often ease into proper perspective during these quiet times.

20

The Written Word

It's a source of amazement and some amusement that many articulate people are reduced to blubbering incompetents when required to put their thoughts on paper.

Some people are intimidated by a blank sheet of paper and a pen (or typewriter). Let's examine why this feeling of panic overtakes individuals who otherwise appear to be competent and confident.

First, we have the *test syndrome*. Some people panic when taking examinations. All they have is that blank sheet of paper and the material inside their head, which must be "up" to translating information to paper. Pass or fail depends on what is scratched on that threatening blank sheet.

Another reason people may not feel confident about using the written word is that they do not read much themselves. They get through what they consider required reading, but they don't read for pleasure. Instead, they watch television, which is more passive than reading. You don't learn much about good writing by watching television. Clearly, television is not to be blamed for all the social ills attributed to it. However, few would quarrel that it has lessened the time spent reading, which in turn has had an adverse effect on many people's interest in writing.

The telephone also plays a part in discouraging the written word. Although most of us (unless we are employed by a phone service) would like to see less expensive phone bills, the fact is that it is relatively inexpensive to make a long distance phone call today. This was not the case for previous generations. A long distance phone call was a luxury most could not afford, if they had a telephone. People wrote letters instead, and it cost only three cents to mail them. Today very few people under age 40 write letters. People communicate with distant friends by telephone. It's a more intimate and satisfying way of communicating, but it has destroyed the art of letter writing.

People who spell poorly are usually aware of the fact and don't want to look foolish by demonstrating it. So they avoid writing. There's an easy solution to this excuse.

Every secretary is familiar with "word books." They are like dictionaries except there are no definitions. You go to a word book to get the correct spelling. It's the reason most people go to the dictionary. A word book is simply more convenient. It's small and easy to hide in the middle drawer of your desk. I'm a better than average speller, but I keep two of them—one at my office and one in my den at home. They remove an obstacle to writing.

Because people don't write much, they are intimidated when they do have to write. An analogy to public speaking might make the point. If you seldom give a speech in public, you are probably intimidated by the situation. And when you are intimidated, you are not relaxed. You are uptight and nervous. Your manner of speaking is stiff and uncomfortable. You communicate your apprehension to the audience; people may even feel uncomfortable for you. Your manner destroys their confidence in you and in the truth or wisdom of the message you are trying to deliver.

The same thing happens with a written communication. If you are intimidated by the situation, your writing will be stiff and stilted. Under such circumstances, you may try to cover the situation by writing in a more formal manner, using words you would never use in conversation with a friend.

Books and courses will tell you how to write business letters and interoffice memos. They can be a big help, provided you don't take on the characteristics of the person who wrote the course. Your goal is to improve your technical skills, not to change your personality.

My suggestion for improving your writing skills is to use

mental imagery. Instead of being intimidated by the blank piece of paper, get a mental image of the person you are writing to. See that person in your mind. You might even go so far as to imagine the person seated in an easy chair at the office drinking a cup of coffee and reading your letter. Or you could visualize yourself sitting in a coffee shop telling the person the message you want to convey.

Imagine that you are having a conversation with the person in a friendly environment. Now speak. Use words you'd use in conversation. If you don't use four-syllable words in your conversation, don't use them in your written communication; they usually denote a feeling of inferiorty. (Even if you do feel inferior about your writing, don't advertise it—keep it to yourself.)

When conjuring up the mental picture of the person you're writing to, always imagine a friendly face. Even if you are writing to someone you can't stand, imagine that you're writing to a friend. *Never* conjure up hostile feelings because they may come through in your writing. Imagining a friendly face will bring a friendly, warm tone to your communication.

Now let's take a broader situation: writing a memo to all the people in your department or division. You don't want to imagine forty-five people sitting in an auditorium waiting for you to speak. That's too formal a situation, and unless you're an outstanding and relaxed public speaker, the image is going to make your writing formal and uptight.

Instead, get a mental picture of two or three of the friendliest subordinates you have reporting to you. Imagine that you are on a coffee break or lunch break with them. Now say to them what you have to say. That's what you write. If you're writing to fellow managers in other departments, you can use similar mental images.

Now, let's assume you have to write a report or a memo to the president of the company, and let's assume you are scared to death of Ms. Big. Getting a mental image of the president is only going to make the situation worse. Think instead of your kindly aunt, the one who is your favorite. Imagine that relative as the president. Now write the letter. The tone will be altogether different.

Incidentally, no matter how informal your organization is, always address the president formally. Never address the president by his first name. At the end of the letter type your full name and title; sign just your first name if you wish. This suggests that although you show respect for the president and the office, you are not a stuffy person who expects such formality in return.

Writing informally does not mean using incomplete sentences or faulty grammer. You need to make certain your grammar is correct. It's the tone of the communication that I am concerned with.

If you are uncomfortable about your use of grammar in written communications, learn the basics. They are not that tough and they are certainly not cumbersome. An inexpensive book on grammar will help you in that regard. Don't rely on a secretary to backstop you in this area. That's the easy way out and may cause you to put off achieving competence in this important skill.

The reason I strongly recommend that your grammar be correct in writing is: If it isn't, there's a chance that it's also incorrect in your formal speaking and even in informal conversations. If that is the case, it may have an adverse impact on future promotion possibilities.

So do your best to write and speak the language correctly and to give it the dignity it deserves. Above all, remember— write to that friendly mental image.

21

The Telephone

Almost all of us have known people who in person are warm and friendly but for some reason sound brusque and un-friendly on the telephone.

You've probably heard the following statement (origin unknown): "You never get a second chance to make a first impression." If you make a bad first impression, who knows how long it may take to overcome it? Unfortunately, you may not know when you're creating a negative impression, especially on the telephone. What follows are some suggestions that may help the first-time manager develop some good phone habits.

Avoid Screening Your Calls

When a person moves into management there is a great temptation to start having all phone calls screened by an assistant. It's usually unnecessary, and is often an ego trip on the part of the new manager to appear important and busy.

Put yourself in the position of the caller. In most organizations the call comes through a switchboard, and the following dialogue occurs:

Operator: Good afternoon, the Acme Company.
Smith: May I speak to Mary Jones, the manager of Accounts Receivable?

Operator: One moment please [*or* I'll ring her].

[The call is put through and your assistant answers.]

Assistant: Ms. Jones's office.
Smith: [*again*]: May I speak to Mary Jones?
Assistant: I'll see if she's in. Who may I say is calling?
Smith: Lloyd Smith.
Assistant: May I tell her what it's about?
Smith: I want to see if she's received my check.

[The assistant comes back on the line in a minute or two.]

Assistant: I'm sorry, she's in a meeting. May I have her call you?

[If the caller isn't exasperated, he probably gives the number. About two hours later, the assistant phones back.]

Assistant: Mr. Smith please.
Smith: This is Lloyd Smith.
Assistant: Would you hold for Ms. Mary Jones? She'll be on the line in just a moment.

If Mr. Smith slams the phone in the assistant's ear, it is just what this egomaniacal procedure deserves.

I'm not suggesting that you always answer your own phone. Obviously if you're away from the area, someone must cover your calls. But when you're at your desk and not in conference, answer the phone when it rings.

Many callers who are asked by the assistant, "Who may I say is calling?" or "May I tell her what it's about?" may take these questions personally. They interpret them this way: "If I'm important enough, or the subject matter is big enough, maybe I'll get through." Unfortunately, that is the way many callers read such questions because many people do get the runaround on the telephone.

Place Calls Yourself

There is hardly any valid reason for having an assistant place phone calls for you. It takes longer for the assistant to place the call and then tell you that the party is on the line than it does to place the call yourself. With redial capabilities and the ability to place frequently called numbers on an automatic dialer, I can think of few reasons to have these calls placed for you.

It may be obvious that if you're going to make a business phone call, you ought to have any necessary file pulled and all required information at hand. The thought might occur to you that having an assistant screening calls provides an opportunity for the appropriate file to be pulled as the call is switched to you. That is true, but the poor impression the screening creates simply isn't worth it.

Every manager ought to have a buzzer connected to an assistant's desk so that when he is on the phone and needs a file pulled, the assistant can get it. Buzz the assistant and write on a pad, "Please pull the R. L. Schultz file." For this purpose, always keep two pads by your phone—one to make your own notes and the other to write notes to your assistant.

When you review your phone messages after having been away from the office or in a meeting, see which ones require the file to be pulled before returning calls. Or, an experienced assistant can do this even before you return.

Telephone Technique

Let's discuss some techniques for making your telephone voice sound warm and friendly.

A pleasant tone of voice is essential; any harshness will create a bad impression. People can't control the voices they were given, but they can practice sounding friendly, efficient, and businesslike. But take care not to go to the other extreme and sound gushy and saccharine sweet—it sounds phony.

Getting into the habit of smiling when you answer the phone will do wonders for your tone of voice. This isn't always easy to do—especially in the middle of a hectic day when the last thing you need is another interruption. But the person calling does not know that it's a bad time to call and does not deserve to be snapped at. Place a small mirror with a stand-up bracket next to your phone so that you can see yourself smile while you're on the phone. (The problem with leaving it on your desk permanently is that people will think you are narcissistic.)

Another way to improve your telephone voice is to have it recorded. A small contact microphone can be purchased at almost any sound or stereo shop for a few dollars. It plugs into the microphone connection on a cassette recorder. With this device in place, have a friend call you several times. Answer the phone in various ways: smiling, frowning, hurried, and so on. You can then hear what you sound like to others on the phone. If you're not used to hearing your recorded voice and are like most people, you probably won't like the way you sound. But if you don't record your voice, you can only guess how you sound, and you'll have no clue about the impression you make. Friends, unwilling to hurt your feelings, are unlikely to tell you if your voice is unpleasant. No matter how bad you think you sound, you can improve your phone voice enough to come across pleasantly on the telephone.

In Your Absence

In addition to your own phone manners and tone of voice, you need to be concerned about how the phone is answered in your absence, and in your area generally. When you are outside the office, call in once in a while to find out how calls are being handled.

A phone call that comes to your office in your absence ought to be answered, "Ms. Abernathy's office" or "Mr. Taylor's office." Even if the style of your office is casual, the phone call may be from someone outside the company, so the more formal approach should be used. If the approach is too casual, the customer may think you will be too casual with his concerns too. How would you like to be wheeled into the surgical suite and hear the janitor greet your surgeon, "Hi-ya Freddie"?

If you are at an early-morning meeting, don't allow your assistant to tell people that you aren't in yet. That makes it look as if you don't get to work on time. Far better for him to say, "Ms. Abernathy had a breakfast meeting downtown this morning." Your assistant should always be told about the meeting the afternoon before an early appointment. How much you want to tell strangers on the phone is a matter of discretion.

Perhaps this is so obvious that it shouldn't be mentioned, but sometimes the more obvious matters are overlooked. When your assistant takes calls in your absence, he must always ask for the phone number. Occasionally, a caller will say, "She knows my number." In that case the assistant shouldn't push for it. Before you return, however, the assistant ought to look up the number on your phone listings.

It is important to indicate the time the call is received. Most managers will look over all their phone messages, sort out the emergencies, and return the rest in the order they were received on a first-come, first-served basis.

22

Learning to Listen

One of the best-kept secrets of successful management is the ability to listen. Most new managers become very concerned about their ability to communicate. Too many managers have the mistaken idea that the minute they are promoted everyone is going to hang on to every word they say. They set out to fill that need. That is exactly the wrong approach. Such managers should remember they have two ears and one mouth; therefore, they ought to do twice as much listening as talking.

Listening is one of the most valuable traits that a new manager can demonstrate, for two important reasons: First, if you do a great deal of listening, you will not be thought of as a know-it-all, which is how most people perceive someone who talks too much. Second, by doing a lot of listening and little talking, you'll learn what is going on. You'll learn none of it by talking.

Most people are not good listeners, and we ought to examine why this is so.

Many people think the most beautiful sound in the world is the sound of their own voice. It's truly music to their ears. They can't get enough of it so they require others to listen to it. Typically, such people are more interested in what they are going to say themselves than in what the other person is saying. I would submit that most people can remember approximately 80 percent of what they said personally and approximately 20 percent of what the other person said. The reason, in my opinion, is that people only partially listen to what the other person is saying. They are too busy thinking of what they are going to say "as soon as this idiot takes a breath and shuts up."

If you don't remember anything else about this chapter, you'll do yourself immeasurable good by remembering this statement: *If you want to be thought of as a brilliant conversationalist, be a good listener.*

Another reason people are not good listeners is the *comprehension gap.* Most people communicate at approximately 100 words per minute, but we have the capacity to comprehend approximately 400 words per minute. So what happens during that 300-word comprehension gap? A speaking speed of 100 words per minute doesn't demand our full attention, so we tend to tune the speaker out and think of other things. Many times we become more interested in what we are thinking about and never tune back to the speaker. How many times has your spouse said to you, "I told you about that two weeks ago. You were not listening to me"? Effectively, your spouse is saying, "You are tuning me out and not tuning me back in." You may have started out listening, but since you were thinking about other things at the crucial time, you didn't hear what you were being told.

Everyone has a need to be listened to. What a wonderful service we provide, therefore, if we are good listeners. The manager who is a good listener fills a great need for every employee on the staff.

People pay large sums of money to be listened to by others—notably, by psychiatrists and psychologists. Some communities have established telephone "crisis lines" to help people with their problems. Some religious organizations have instituted prayer hot lines staffed by people who listen to callers and then pray with them. Further evidence of people's great need for listeners is the phenomenal growth of call-in radio shows, in which the caller's comments are aired live or on a delayed broadcast to a large listening audience.

One radio station uses the delayed broadcast to great advantage. Announcers report during the day that their "hot line" or "talk line" is now open. They further announce what the topic is or state that "today it's a random topic—whatever you want to talk about." They also announce that the show will be played "at 10:30 tonight." People call in, expound to their heart's content, and then tune in at night to listen to the radio station. This fills two great needs in such people. It fills their need to have someone listen to them and it also fills their need to hear themselves—"the most beautiful sound in the world."

The people who call these radio stations often comment on what a great service the station is performing. It may be that they can't get their spouses, children, or friends to listen to them. But if hundreds of thousands or even millions of strangers will listen to them, at least part of the great need to be listened to is fulfilled.

Ego is another reason many people have trouble becoming good listeners. They have the mistaken notion that they are subjugating themselves to others by listening—that if they're not dominating the conversation, they're in an inferior position. Actually, the person doing the listening has more control than the talker. The talker desperately needs the listener. The listener doesn't need the talker; there are millions of talkers to take his place. Listeners are in great demand; talkers are a dime a dozen.

Good listeners possess several traits, all of which can be developed. For one thing, they encourage the other person to talk. When listeners do talk, they don't turn the conversation back to themselves. They continue the line of talk of the other person. They use certain phrases or gestures to signal to the talker that they are truly interested in what she has to say.

Looking at someone who is talking to you indicates that you're interested in what he has to say—that, in fact, you are hanging on every word. Nodding your head affirmatively every once in a while indicates that you understand what the talker is saying. Smiling at the same time indicates that you are enjoying the conversation.

A well-placed comment also indicates to the talker that you have a genuine interest in what he has to say.

"That's interesting."
"Tell me more."

"Why do you suppose she said that?"
"Why did you feel that way?"

As a matter of fact, just saying "That's interesting; tell me more" will make you a brilliant conversationalist in the minds of everyone with whom you come in contact.

People enjoy being around someone who shows a genuine interest in them. Good listening skills carry over into many aspects of both your professional and personal life. The interesting thing is that you can start out using these techniques because you realize people will like being with you. There's nothing wrong with such an attitude. You become well liked and your subordinates get a manager who makes them feel good about themselves.

Everyone gains from such an arrangement. You may have to work on your human relations skills, but eventually they'll become second nature. At first you may consider such behavior to be role playing. But after a while you'll be unable to tell when the role playing has stopped and it's actually you. You'll derive a great deal of personal satisfaction from being the kind of person others enjoy being around. You'll also be a much more effective manager.

23

A Sense of Humor: A Trusted Friend

Many new managers take themselves much too seriously. Life is earnest, life is grim, and without a sense of humor, it is deadly. New managers have to learn not to take themselves too seriously and to develop a sense of humor.

One reason many of us take ourselves too seriously is because of the immediacy of the world in which we move. Our daily activities are important to us because they're the ones we know most intimately. Therefore, everything that happens at the office looms large in our lives. We should try to do our jobs to the best of our ability, but once we're sure in our own minds that we have done so, we shouldn't worry about it. The key phrase is *once we're sure in our own minds*. Most of us are our own severest critics.

Of course the work we do is important. If it were not, no one would part with cold cash in return for our efforts. But we must keep what we do in perspective. It may be important in our office, and it may be important to the people who deal with our office, but it may not seem terribly significant when measured against the history of humankind. When you've had a bad day and all seems lost, remember that a hundred years from now no one will care, so why should you let it ruin your year, month, week—or evening, for that matter? Our jobs are important, but let's keep what we do in perspective.

One of my favorite quotes, by the English author Horace

Walpole (1717–1797), is "The world is a comedy to those that think, a tragedy to those that feel."

It's much easier not to take yourself too seriously if you have a sense of humor. Nearly everyone has some sort of sense of humor. But it is more keenly developed in some people than in others. Even if you feel your sense of humor is weak, you can improve it.

Developing a Sense of Humor

Here's a news flash that provides some hope. Many people who have a reputation for being funny, clever, and humorously creative don't really have any of these characteristics. What they have is a terrific memory and a sense of *appropriateness recall*. They can reach back into their memories quickly and find a humorous line they've heard or read that's appropriate to the situation at hand. They get a reputation for having a sense of humor, and they do have one, but they're not necessarily creative. It's much like the difference between perfect pitch, which some feel a person is born with, and relative pitch, which can be developed and practiced.

So you can develop a sense of humor by reading, by seeing the right kind of humorous movies, and by studying comedy. Watch television personalities who have a reputation for being funny. Watch people who are "ear funny." A cream pie in the face or a pratfall might be "sight funny," but you can't use these gags at the office, and seldom in your social life.

When my younger brother, Gene, was graduating from high school, he commented that with a couple hundred in his graduating class, nothing would set him apart from his classmates. I had a suggestion: "As you walk across the stage, stumble and fall on your face just as you get close to the area where you're handed your diploma. You'll get a big laugh, and you'll be fondly remembered at every class reunion for the rest of your life."

Fortunately, Gene did not take my advice, but he was thinking about it as he walked across the stage, and as a result he was grinning from ear to ear. That alone set him apart from most of the other graduates.

Humor—Not Sarcasm

Achieving a reputation for having a dry sense of humor is acceptable; acquiring a reputation as the office clown is not. I'm sure you appreciate the difference. Being witty is one thing; being a buffoon is quite another. But one warning: If you have never said anything funny at the office, break into humor on a gradual basis; otherwise someone will want to check the water supply.

Many people mistake sarcasm for wit; some sarcasm can be funny, but there's a twofold problem with being sarcastic. First, you achieve a reputation for being a cynic, which is not a welcome trait in the executive suite. Second, sarcasm is often funny at someone else's expense. You don't want people to think you prey on the weaknesses or idiosyncrasies of others. Also you don't want to offend someone and make an enemy. It's best if your humorous remarks point inward or are neutral in nature. Making fun of yourself or your own foibles makes you a self-deprecating wit, which offends no one. Trading insults with another person can be fun, but it's not a practice for beginners and therefore should be avoided.

Humor, the Tension Reliever

A sense of humor is most valuable when things become hectic and tense. A well-placed humorous remark can relieve the tension. It's like opening a steam valve so that the pressure can escape. It's healthy to see humor in tense situations. Even when it seems inappropriate to make your humorous remark aloud, thinking about it may put a smile on your face and keep you from getting a migraine.

We are surrounded by funny situations every day, but it takes a trained eye to see them. As with the beauty all around us, we don't look for them, and we may not even recognize them when we do see them. With practice, however, you'll begin to see the humor in what goes on all around you.

Finally, there's a compelling reason for not taking ourselves and this life too seriously: None of us is going to get out of it alive anyway.

24

Managing, Participating in, and Leading Meetings

In Chapter 19, mention was made of companies that have "closed periods" during which office personnel don't phone one another and don't attend meetings. That gives them a certain amount of uninterruptible time each day. Indeed, I have often thought the productivity of the entire country would be greatly increased if all office meetings of more than two people, in business and government, were banned for one year.

The Meeting Surrogate

Another suggestion is that each company designate a few people as professional meeting attenders—surrogates for everyone else in the office. One person might be a surrogate for twenty managers and executives. Every time you're summoned to a meeting, you could send your surrogate; then, if anything important happened (which, of course, is highly unlikely), the surrogate could condense it and report it back to you. The only people who would fail to see both the value and the humor in such a proposal are those who like to go to meetings.

People who like to go to meetings are easily identifiable. They're the ones who do most of the talking and wander off the topic as a means of prolonging the meeting. An additional benefit for them in the ploy is that it delays their having to go back to work, where their progress might be measured. This type of person should be selected as one of the meeting surrogates.

The idea of the meeting surrogate is so radical and yet so practical that it will not be adopted in our lifetime, so we'd all better face up to the hard reality of having to attend some meetings.

Advance Notice

Another proposal that might be considered bold is to announce the agenda of a meeting in advance. That would give people a chance to prepare somewhat for the meeting. But such a procedure would require a chairperson who has a lot of charity in his or her makeup. Some people chairing a meeting need to feel superior, and they can achieve that goal only if they alone know what's going to be discussed.

Whenever possible, find out what's going to be considered at the meeting, what decisions will be made, and come prepared. Ask yourself:

"What information do I need to vote intelligently on the required decisions? In what way can my particular experiences with the company provide valuable input to the entire committee? What points of view are the other members of the committee likely to bring to the meeting? Is the chairperson's point of view likely to prevail? Do I agree or disagree with it? Do I have a strong opinion on the subject, or do I need a lot more facts? Am I completely neutral on the issue? Are certain people on the committee going to fight for their position or is the entire committee likely to be neutral until the facts come out and the discussion develops?"

Mistakes Managers Make

There's one compulsion that many managers too readily give in to at meetings: They feel obligated to say something, assuming that their silence will be interpreted as ignorance. In the words of the old saw, "It's better to remain silent and be thought a fool than to open your mouth and remove all doubt." Obviously, you can't sit in stony silence throughout the entire meeting, but you shouldn't feel compelled to speak just for the sake of saying something.

How you handle yourself in the first few meetings you attend will create either a positive or negative impression that many of the other participants will carry with them for quite a while. You'd be well advised to choose your statements at the first few meetings quite carefully. If what you say is well thought out and adds insight leading toward solution of the problem, you'll carry far more weight than if you merely try to be agreeable and utter a lot of insignificant prattle such as "I sure agree with that"; "That's interesting"; "I'm sure most people haven't thought of it that way"; "That's right; that's for sure."

Another mistake I've seen new managers make in meetings with other executives is to seize the first opportunity to say something uncomplimentary about a subordinate. This inclines me strongly to the view that such people may not have been ready for management. They doubtless expect and possibly even demand loyalty from their own staff; they clearly owe the same loyalty to their subordinates. Loyalty and respect have to move in both directions, or it won't be long before they fail to exist in either direction.

You don't gain anything in the eyes of your peers if you knock one of your subordinates. If you're in a situation where frank assessment of an employee's performance is imperative, then you'll want to be completely honest in your appraisal. But a remark such as "I've got a couple of real deadheads in my department in Louie and Joe" is inappropriate. While the statement doesn't do Louie and Joe any good, it harms the person who makes it most of all.

Keeping Your Cool

One rule to fix firmly in yourself as a behavior pattern is never to lose your cool in a meeting. Unfortunately, every company

has executives who use meetings to make provocative statements that are designed to get under the skin of others. Some
of them do it unconsciously, never realizing they're creating
turmoil. Those who do it deliberately are compulsive mischief
makers who like to keep things stirred up. Some of your peers
and superiors perhaps enjoy testing you to see what it takes to
get you to lose your cool. The ability to hold your own in such
situations will stand you in good stead in all aspects of your
management career.

One critical test in this area will come the first time someone in a meeting indicates that part or all of a certain problem
derives from lack of performance in your department. Your
spontaneous reaction might be, "Like hell it is! You're out of
your mind!" That's the wrong way to react, even though it's
perfectly natural and completely understandable. You'd be
much better off responding, "I suppose that's possible. Maybe
you know something about my department I don't know. I'd
be interested in some facts and figures."

Usually, the more defensive you are when someone makes
a statement about your area of responsibility, the more inclined
people will be to believe the charge is justified. However, if it
doesn't seem to shake you up, if you seem to be completely in
control, they'll wonder about the veracity of the statement. If
you're sure of what the situation is and you know your adver-
sary is incorrect, you can remain cool because you know what
the outcome will be. Any kind of investigation of the facts will
support your position. It's more difficult to remain believable
and look confident if you lose your cool and become defensive.

Of course, there are people who'll accuse you of being
defensive when all you're doing is answering the question.
They do it because they know how people hate being called
defensive in an office situation. It has the aspects of a self-
fulfilling prophecy. You're not being defensive, but when
someone accuses you of being defensive, you sound defensive
while denying it.

I believe your best best is always to come down on the side
of understatement rather than overstatement. If you oversell
your point of view, it may come back to haunt you. You're
much better off selling your point of view logically, in easily

understandable terms. When you sell it emotionally, the support you receive can float away on another wave of emotion that takes an opposite course. If you can explain your position rationally, and document the case you make for it, that support will not so readily be lost to you.

There's another compelling reason for remaining cool and in control. Your superiors on the committee will see your demeanor, and you may achieve a reputation for "coolness under fire"—a desirable trait for anyone moving up the corporate ladder.

Not only in meetings but in the entire managerial process, people too often tend to work backward. They make the decision that gratifies them emotionally and then dig out facts and figures they need to justify the decision logically. Don't fool yourself. You'll occasionally make an emotional decision, but don't kid yourself into believing you arrived at it logically. You'll of course make some decisions that are both emotional and logical; the ones that can get you in trouble are those that are emotional and lacking in logic.

All of us make emotional decisions on occasion. Show me an executive who never makes an emotional decision and I'll show you either a robot or a person who has perfected rationalization into an exact science.

Yes-Men (Male or Female)

Another problem that's characteristic of meetings is the tendency for the yes-man (male or female) to surface. This will happen primarily when the meeting includes executives holding various ranks on the organization chart. As a student of human nature, you'll see both subtle and not so subtle forms of obsequiousness on the part of yes-men in your organization—perhaps the word *brownnosing* won't seem out of place to describe such odious behavior.

We must be completely honest with each other. The reason there are yes-men is because some people believe it pays off. It doesn't matter to some that the price being paid for advancement is too high. Then there are those who prostitute themselves in a business situation so regularly that they don't even know they're doing it.

This is an area where I must be careful in advising you. My impulses tend to carry me in the opposite direction: Even when I agree with the boss, I'm reluctant to show it because I don't like even the appearance of being a yes-man. But that extreme is bad too. It's almost reverse snobbery. Ideally, you should openly agree with your boss when you do honestly agree, and disagree when that's what you truly feel. You're in trouble if you have a boss who speaks loudly against being surrounded by a bunch of yes-men but who doesn't take kindly to disagreement. It's not what is said, it's what the action proves. To paraphrase Ralph Waldo Emerson: Your actions speak so loudly, I can't hear what you're saying.

Frankly, if the company you're with is one that fosters yes-man behavior up and down the organization chart, then I suggest you consider leaving, because there's no way you can survive in a place like that without selling your soul. Some things are more important than getting promoted or receiving a raise—maintaining your integrity, for example. If your integrity can be bought for a promotion or a raise, then you don't have any, baby!—integrity, that is.

It's fairly easy to pick out the yes-men (male or female) in a meeting. They're the ones who glance up and down the table to check out the lay of the land before committing themselves. Then, when they do speak, their statements are so tentative or ambiguous that, should a superior start to disagree, they have only to make a slight shift in their position to be completely in accord with the higher authority.

People like that are worthless at a meeting. Unfortunately, some executives like being surrounded by such completely predictable subordinates who believe what the boss believes. On the other hand, I've seen really sharp executives putting potential yes-men through some of the most intricate tap dancing and sidestepping you can imagine. These executives are so sure of themselves that they'll change their own position 180 degrees during a long meeting just to see how far the yes-men will go with them. The terminal cases go with them all the way.

If you're going to make a contribution to a meeting, then you have to be in a secure enough position to say what you think. If that can't occur, there's no sense in being part of that committee or group.

Refusing to Go Along With the Crowd

When you feel compelled to disagree with other people or with a committee, do it in a diplomatic way. The person you're disagreeing with isn't wrong—it's the position taken by that person that's incorrect. Keep that always in mind and you'll get along much better than if you have people believing you're going after them personally. Unfortunately, you'll find there are people who take any disagreement as personal. That's their particular personality quirk and there's nothing you can do about it, except to make sure in your own mind that it's not personal with you.

Another mistake made by people new to management or attending meetings has to do with their reaction to questions they can't answer. There's a temptation to bluff your way through that kind of situation. You'll usually be found out if you do this too often. It's best to say, "I'm not sure" or "I don't know." If you bluff, you're likely to give a wrong answer and thereby create even more problems.

When you're new in your position, your "I don't know" will be tolerated for a while. However, with time that protective "I don't know" ought to diminish greatly. And it will, as you achieve a better understanding of your job and know what you're doing.

One of my wishes for you is that you don't spend an inordinate amount of time going to a great variety of meetings. They cut into your productive time. Most committee meetings don't accomplish much. I often get the feeling that committees were invented as a method of "spreading the blame" for decisions that may be unpopular. I see nothing wrong with asking to be excused from a meeting when you believe you have higher-priority items to work on. You can't do it too often, but once in a while it'll work.

As you approach a meeting, set your emotions at a high frustration level. For example, one great frustration is having to spend a lot of time in a meeting whose purpose seems insignificant compared with the more important things waiting for you in your office. As you "do time" in a corporation, especially if you're in a large office, you'll find many things that frustrate you. If you don't learn to handle these frustrations, you'll get ulcers, high blood pressure, or worse.

With a bit of practice you can learn to be "alone" even in a crowd. You can actually build a protective psychological shield around yourself, so that even if you see the frustration possibilities building up, you've developed a toughness that they bounce harmlessly off of. You're aware of them, but they don't get through to you. It's a kind of toughness that says, "I am the master of my fate: I am the captain of my soul." This ability will be of value beyond your meetings. You decide what filters through to you. You're aware of what's going on, but you decide where you'll allow your emotions to get involved.

Chairing a Committee

In your role as a new manager, the chances are remote that you'll be made chairperson of a permanent committee. However, you may end up as chairperson of a special task force or of a subcommittee. The best training for chairing a committee is participation in committee activities and the ordeal of suffering through meetings that are badly run. If you've never attended a well-run committee meeting, you might not fully appreciate what you're missing. Some managers spend their entire business life without ever having attended a well-run meeting.

You can run a well-organized meeting that gets through its business with dispatch and still be a rotten chairperson. It seems to me that there are two extremes. One is the chairperson who allows the meeting to drift through irrelevant topics for long periods and who generally lacks control. In this case, the meeting takes much too long for the business at hand. The other extreme is the dictatorial chairperson who has so much clout in the organization that no one on the committee can buck him or her. Such people know what they want done, and they tolerate no major disagreement. They get a meeting over with quickly. It may be a rubber-stamp committee, but it's efficient. Obviously, we want to be somewhere between these two extremes.

Certain Basics

There are certain basics you should remember if you're going to be successful at presiding over meetings. The fundamental responsibility of a presiding officer is to conduct the business of the committee with fairness and dispatch, allowing all members an opportunity to participate in the deliberations. Most committees within a company are run informally; you'll seldom chair a committee that requires you to be an expert parliamentarian. (In that event, of course, you'll have to become familiar with those more technical approaches.)

As chairperson, you should see that everyone receives an agenda well in advance of the meeting. This will give members the opportunity to prepare themselves for the questions and issues to be considered. The timing of the agenda depends on the frequency of the meetings. If you meet monthly, distributing the agenda about ten days in advance should be sufficient. If you meet weekly, you can have some mutually agreed upon time for distributing both the minutes of the past meeting and the agenda of the coming meeting.

All agendas show the starting time of the meeting. It adds discipline to the meeting if you also show the proposed closing time. People tend to stay focused on the subject if they can anticipate the ending time. There's less tendency to "wander off."

Distributing the minutes to people before the meeting can be quite a time-saver. Committee members will read the minutes before the next meeting. If you go through the formality of approving the minutes, there'll usually be a motion to approve the minutes as published. The only exception is when a member feels that a correction in the minutes is necessary. These corrections are usually minor.

Another advantage of having an agenda is its disciplinary effect on the entire committee. Members know what their objectives are. You'll usually get no static if you always provide a spot on your agenda for "other business." This gives members an opportunity to discuss whatever other items they think should be considered by the committee. It also says to committee members, "We'll take up other business after we've disposed of these first priorities."

As chairperson, you should let members know they can request that items be added to the agenda. I favor identifying these requests by the person making them. This saves you time because if other committee members want additional information about the particular agenda item added, say, by Mr. Smith, they'll call Mr. Smith instead of you, the chairperson.

Before the meeting begins, people will usually be carrying on various private conversations. Calling the meeting to order is therefore necessary. It can usually be done by speaking in a louder voice, or tapping a coffee cup with a spoon and saying, "Shall we get started?" If it's a more formal setting, you might say, "Can we come to order, please?"

Keep the committee on the subject. Committees have a way of drifting away from the business at hand. The chairperson must be a diplomat in keeping members attentive to the task in front of them. Your repertoire should include statements like this:

"That's very interesting, Fred. How does that tie back into our discussion of agenda item number six?"

"I'm afraid we're drifting away from the subject. Even though this is very interesting, we'd better get back to our agenda."

"We're beginning to make some of the same arguments for the second and third time. Are we ready to make a decision on this matter?"

"I don't want to discourage a complete discussion on this, but the hour is getting late, and we still have much material to cover."

One problem a new manager may encounter is in chairing a committee that consists of some executives in the organization who outrank him or her. Sometimes the manager looks to that ranking executive for major leadership on the committee. If the company had wanted that executive to be the dominant force on the committee, he would have been designated as chairperson instead of you.

The most uncomfortable situation for a new manager is when the president sits on the committee. It's difficult to treat that officer like any other member, but I think you have to stay as close to that posture as possible. Obviously, if the president wants to digress from the agenda for any reason, it isn't too smart to say, "Let's get back to the agenda." In most companies, the president won't be the problem. The problem will be other members of the committee who are trying to impress the top executive.

Most organizations are not going to put you in the position of chairing a committee consisting of people who outrank you. You'll usually chair a committee consisting of peers and a few subordinates.

The rules of common sense should prevail in chairing meetings. Keep your cool. Don't let anyone press your panic button. Be courteous to everyone on the committee. Avoid putting anyone down. Always deal with the problem at hand—don't get involved in personalities, no matter how much anyone else does. Be better organized than anyone else on the committee. Develop the kind of trustful relationship with people on the committee that will prompt them always to come to you beforehand with unusual items for the group, thereby avoiding unpleasant surprises. Be fair to everyone, even those whose viewpoints you disagree with.

I believe you can do a better job of building this kind of relationship with committee members if as chairperson you vote only to break ties. I know of government committees that require a roll-call vote from everyone, including the chairperson. I see no need for this in a business situation. Avoid it.

You can be fair and considerate and still leave no doubt as to who's in charge and running the meeting. If you're fair to all viewpoints, you'll have the respect of the entire committee. At times one or two members will argue a position that the majority becomes impatient with; the fair chairperson will see that minority opinions are heard and will not allow the majority to overwhelm the dissenters. If you handle the controversy properly, you'll get the respect of members of the majority because they know on some other issue they might hold a minority position.

Being a successful committee chairperson is another opportunity to demonstrate the quality of your management skills.

25

Learning to Be an
Adequate Public Speaker

I'm repeatedly amazed by the number of capable executives who can't handle a public speaking situation. Standing up there on the platform, they come off as the dullest clods imaginable. The impression the audience gets of them is that they're not very good on the job either.

Prior Preparation

Many managers are rotten public speakers because they wait until they find themselves in a speaking situation before they do anything about it. By then it's too late. You can be the greatest manager in the world and your light will be hidden under a bushel basket if you don't prepare yourself to be a public speaker.

Because so few people in managerial positions prepare themselves to speak publicly, you'll have a leg up on most of them if you learn how it's done. Public speaking frightens many people, and so they avoid it like the plague. But what they probably don't consider early in their careers is that although speeches to outside groups may be avoided, the speech that will take place within their own office must be faced.

It may be a meeting of your department in which you have

to get up and explain some new company policy. It may be a retirement dinner for someone in your area of responsibility, and you're expected to make a "few appropriate remarks." I've seen managers go to unbelievable lengths to avoid such speaking situations. They will use ploys such as arranging a business trip so they'll be out of town or scheduling their own vacation for that time. They'll spend the rest of their business lives plotting how not to get up in front of a group and speak. How much better off they'd be if they'd obtain the necessary skills and turn these negative situations into resounding pluses.

What many people don't realize is that learning to be an adequate public speaker will also improve their ability to speak extemporaneously. How do you respond when you're unexpectedly called on to say a few words? The most extreme example of someone who has difficulty in front of an audience is the person "who couldn't lead a group in silent prayer."

The close friend who first got me interested in public speaking is fond of saying, "Speech training won't get rid of the butterflies in your stomach, but it will organize them into effective squadrons."

Toastmasters International

It seems appropriate at this point to mention a nonprofit organization that I believe will help you learn how to be a capable public speaker. I'm referring to Toastmasters International, a self-help organization dedicated to the concept of developing skills in listening, thinking, and speaking. There are neither professionals nor staff members in these clubs, only people who have a mutual interest in developing their speaking capacity. For a modest semiannual fee, you receive the manuals you'll need to begin the process. You go at your own speed, and you'll find a group of people who help one another not only by providing an audience but also by engaging in formal evaluation sessions.

Another aspect of the Toastmasters training that I think is invaluable is what is called "Table Topics." This part of the meeting is designed to develop your skills in extemporaneous speaking. The Topic Master calls on various people (usually those not scheduled to give a formal speech that evening) to talk for two or three minutes on a surprise subject. The time you have to prepare extends from the moment you rise from your chair until the moment you arrive at the lectern.

There are Toastmasters clubs all over the world, so it's likely that you'll find one in your area. If not, you can write to get information about a club close to you. The world headquarters address is Toastmasters International, 2200 N. Grand Avenue, Santa Ana, California 92711.

Obviously, since these clubs include all kinds of individuals, you'll find degrees of quality. But you'll probably gain benefit in direct proportion to the effort you put into it. Most of these clubs meet weekly. Some are dinner clubs and some are not. Naturally, the dinner clubs will cost more.

There are other ways to get speech training. My recommendation of Toastmasters does not exclude other organizations that can help you get the job done. For example, certain community colleges offer training in public speaking. Your desire to obtain these skills is the most important ingredient. Most of the people in your company will be too lazy to go out and seek this training. They'd then have to get off their butts and away from the TV set one night each week. They'd like to be smooth public speakers if they could swallow a vitamin pill once a week, but if it's going to require any effort—forget it.

Fringe Benefits

How many outstanding public speakers do you personally know, either inside or outside your organization? I'll bet not many, if any. Why don't you resolve to be one of the few who are outstanding? Think of the possibilities not only for promotion within your company but for positions of leadership within the community. As a matter of fact, the opportunities for leadership challenges may come more quickly outside the company. Consider what that may open up for you. There are a lot of followers out there waiting for someone to lead them. One characteristic most outstanding leaders have is the ability to speak persuasively on public occasions. There's no reason why you can't be one of those few leaders. You don't have to be brighter than everyone else. There'll always be someone with more smarts than you, but it won't do him or her as much good if you excel in your ability to communicate.

Conclusion

I've covered a variety of topics in this book on how to lead people, but certainly not every situation you'll confront in your career as a manager—or even within the first few weeks in your new role.

There's no way that a book of this sort can be made all-inclusive. I can only hope that I've given you some insight into the techniques of managing people that will make the job more meaningful and understandable. You may think that I've spent an inordinate amount of time on attitudes, on how you view yourself and the problems you face, but that's exactly where your success or failure in working with people will be determined—in your head.

If you're the type of person who believes you're primarily controlled by events, then what's the use? You're then merely a puppet with some giant puppet master pulling the strings. But in actuality it's not that way. Although events beyond your control do have an impact on your life, you control how and what you think. That in turn controls your reaction to these events.

I haven't conned you in this book. I haven't told you that if you work hard and keep your nose clean you'll rise to the top. However, I do think you'll have a better chance if you follow some of these concepts than if you ignore what to me are basic truths. You didn't come into this world with any guarantee that everything would be fair and that the deserving would always get what they deserve. They don't! However, you obviously have no chance to achieve your goals if you just sit there and wait for lightning to strike.

We must grow. This book is devoted to exploring how you manage your people, but I'm just as interested in seeing you grow as a total person. I believe your career can add to your total growth, since it's such a large part of your life. We shouldn't work at a job we don't like, but on the other hand we must be realistic in recognizing that all careers contain aspects we don't like. It's the balance that's important. If most of the job is enjoyable, ego-satisfying, and challenging, then you can put up with the few parts you don't care for. If it's the other way around and you dislike most of what you have to do, you're obviously in the wrong career and you ought to change it. Life is too short to spend time and energy in a career that destroys you.

I have known people, and perhaps you have too, who'll stick with a job they don't like because someday it will provide a great retirement benefit. What good does that prospective retirement benefit do if people ruin their health before they get to retirement? What's worse, they might not live that long.

There are also people around who will complain about a job constantly but will never seek a better job because their fear of change or the unknown is more powerful than their dislike of the job. Some people prefer the predictable even if it's bad than something new or unkown.

Perhaps Abraham Lincoln was right when he said, "Most people are about as happy as they make up their minds to be." That summarizes what I've tried to say throughout this book about the primacy of attitudes.

Too many people, as they approach their middle years, start thinking in terms of the kind of contribution they're making to the world. They often become depressed because they believe what they're doing is not very important. They ask themselves, "How significant is it that I'm a manager in a company making bolts?" Put in that context, it may not seem terribly relevant. But the question that should be asked is, "What kind of impact am I having on the people I come in contact with, both in my work and in my personal life?"

If you can answer that question in a positive way, then it doesn't matter if the company you're associated with is making bolts or life-saving medicine. The system isn't the payoff; the product isn't the payoff; your impact on the people whose lives you touch is what's important. Also, holding a position that's a little higher on the organization chart *does not* make you more important than they are. An executive or a manager is a combination of leader and servant. Not many executives are willing to accept the servant aspect of their responsibilities, because it interferes with their exalted opinion of their rank.

In developing systems for your people to use, you're in fact serving them. In maintaining a salary administration and performance appraisal system, you're serving them. In working out vacation schedules that will allow your people to maximize the benefits of their relaxation time, you're serving them. In hiring and training quality people for your department, you're serving the people who are already there.

Most people have no difficulty understanding the proposition that the President of the United States has immense power but is also a servant—in fact, the number one public servant. The same concept applies to managerial jobs. There's a combination of what appear to be contradictory concepts: authority and a responsibility to serve. If you can keep these in some semblance of balance, I think you'll avoid getting an inflated view of your own importance. You'll also do a better job.

You don't necessarily get smarter. You gain more experience, which many people mistake for wisdom. It doesn't matter what you call it as long as you continually become more effective. You become more effective as you develop a greater variety of experiences in working with people. You gain little from repeating the same experiences except a smoothness that might not otherwise develop.

And the point, although elementary, bears repetition: There's a great deal to be gained from developing empathy for your subordinates' attitudes and feelings. Can you really sense how you'd want to be treated if you were in their position?

I truly wish the best for you as you direct people in what

amounts to nearly one-half of their waking hours. Your success as a manager starts with you and your attitude toward that responsibility. If this book has been of some help to you, then its author is deeply gratified.

A Potpourri of Management Thought Provokers

Don't be afraid to hire people who are smarter than you are. They make you look good, and you achieve a reputation as a judge of talent.

You don't get smarter just because you're promoted. You're the same person you were the day before.

You have two ears and one mouth; therefore you ought to do twice as much listening as talking.

The people who report to you are far more important to your future than the people you report to. Those reporting to you will push you up with their outstanding performance. Those above you will not pull you up if the performance is substandard.

Never become irreplaceable. If you do, you become un-promotable.

If you and I always agree, one of us is unnecessary.

Never take a client to a restaurant named "Mom's."

To not decide is to decide.

You can't lead by pushing.

Never accept credit for something done by a subordinate. It's morally corrupt.

When you criticize subordinates, they may do better because they "have to." When you praise, they do better because they "want to."

When the climate in an organization causes people to play the game of protecting their backsides, creativity goes out the window. Creativity requires taking risks. It's impossible to take risks while looking at your backside in the rearview mirror.

Strange as it may seem, some people prefer predictability, even if it's unpleasant, to risk taking that could lead to improvement.

The world is full of people who want success as long as achieving it creates no inconvenience.

Don't worry if some things are broken once in a while. Even grass grows through cracks.

On rare occasions doing nothing is the right thing to do. It makes you look thoughtful and nonimpulsive.

Treat your people the way you want your boss to treat you.

You are not more important than your subordinates. You just have different responsibilities.

Nearly every salary increase you receive comes at least one year after it was deserved.

There's nothing wrong with being ambitious. The crucial question is "why" you want it.

Not everyone wants to move into management.

If you have a problem with one or two employees violating some company rule, don't take the coward's way out by writing a memo to the entire staff. Why paint the innocent with the guilty brush? Deal directly with the offenders.

One of the biggest complaints employees have about their managers is lack of appreciation for what they do.

When an employee complains about salary, there's a good chance that something else is the cause of dissatisfaction. They're translating it into a money problem, with the attitude, "I'm not being paid enough money to put up with this." Therefore don't take a money complaint at face value without doing some probing.

Never threaten to fire an employee for lack of performance, unless you're prepared to do it.

Never correct or chastise an employee if you're angry, or sorely irritated. Wait until you calm down.

Employees want consistency of behavior from their managers. If they had to choose between a Grouch and a Jekyll-and-Hyde personality, I suspect they'd select the Grouch every time. At least the Grouch is consistent.

Never discuss one employee's shortcomings with another staffer. Once you get the reputation as a "loose lip," you've lost all trust and confidence.

The best way to receive loyalty is to give it.

Some employees who gripe all the time are happiest in their unhappiness. If they didn't have something to complain about, they'd have to face their own personality.

Practice does not make perfect if you're practicing the wrong things.

There's nothing so positive as being negative about a bad idea.

The ultimate diplomacy is the ability to tell the boss that he or she is mistaken.

Admitting there's much you don't know is one of the first acts of maturity.

Admitting you've been mistaken completely disarms most people, as they're used to rationalization and defensiveness.

Knowledge in the human mind without the capacity to use it is like an unread book.

No one of us is as smart as all of us.

The ultimate expert is one who knows more and more about less and less, until he knows everything about nothing.

While we cannot always control what happens, we can control how we react to what happens.

The greatest limitation placed upon us is usually in our own minds.

Some people don't believe they deserve success.

Life, like sport, enables us to raise our level of performance, if we associate with people who are better than we are.

Occasionally, you'll receive credit for something you don't deserve, but not in proportion to the credit you deserve but never receive.

Many people will not apologize because they feel it's a

sign of weakness. Actually it's a sign of character winning out over pettiness.

If someone else won't move off a position, it's a sign of stubborness. When you do it, it's conviction.

When the other person talks too much, he's a "motor mouth." When you do it, you're articulate.

When other people hold back their feelings, they're sullen. When you do it, you're reflective.

When the other person cuts someone up, she's insensitive and sarcastic. When you do it, you're just kidding around.

You can accomplish a great deal if you don't spend an inordinate amount of time worrying about who will get the credit.

You can never build yourself up by tearing down others.

No matter how much money you make, a few hundred dollars more per month would sure make life more comfortable. Even after you receive it, this axiom will still be true.

Some people have an infinite capacity for fooling themselves.

Our schooling may end, but our education never should.

Sometimes a bad decision is better than no decision. At least it gets things moving again.

Carrying a grudge can get to be exceedingly heavy baggage.

The most important characteristic to search for in a job applicant, and the one least looked for, is "attitude."

Our definition of success is often wrong. Too often we define success by what we've accumulated, rather than by what we've become.

Index